MW00535157

KOREAN
HOME
COOKING

JINA JUNG

PHOTOGRAPHS BY AKIKO IDA

KOREAN HOME COOKING

100 authentic everyday recipes,
from bulgogi to bibimbap

murdoch books

Sydney | London

My Korean Kitchen

For me, cooking is much more than a means of survival or a source of pleasure. It's a living witness to history and culture through the taste, presentation and enjoyment of food.

Korean culinary culture was handed down to me by my grandmother and my mother. As a child in Korea, I still remember the mountains of cabbage that filled our living room once a year to prepare kimchi as a family, chillies drying in the sun and the peculiar smell of fermenting soy that would, in a few months, turn into delicious doenjang paste. The mantras of the women in my family still resonate in me when I cook: the order of ingredients, the completeness of colours and the balance of chilli in a dish.

Contrary to popular belief, Korean cuisine is simple.

More than anything, it is an art of living. A traditional Korean meal, as we share it, is composed of several small dishes, meaning that people can come and go as they please.

In this book, you will find a wide variety of traditional, simple and tasty family recipes as well as all the secrets for cooking them at home. You will also have the opportunity to learn new techniques, such as homemade fermentation, and discover new ingredients that you will easily find in specialised grocery stores or order online.

So, take the plunge, come into my kitchen and learn to prepare delicious Korean meals at home.

Jina Jung

RICE
밥

*When I was a girl, my grandfather used to tell me:
'Finish your rice to the last grain, thinking of
the efforts of those who grow it.'*

White rice

HEENBAP

흰 밥

SERVES 4

Preparation 5 minutes
Resting 45 minutes
Cooking 20 minutes

INGREDIENTS

350 g (12 oz) short-grain
  white rice
500 ml (2 cups) water

Put the rice in a bowl and cover with water. Mix lightly using your hand. Empty the water for the first time. Repeat the process twice. Place the rice in a Dutch oven and cover with the 500 ml (2 cups) water. Leave to soak for 30 minutes.

Cover the Dutch oven and heat over a high heat for 10 minutes. When it first comes to the boil, open the lid for a few seconds to prevent it from overflowing and then close again. Repeat this process for the next three times it boils. If the pan looks like it will overflow, then reduce the heat to low, leaving covered. Cook for 10 minutes before turning off the heat. Stand for 15 minutes, covered, before serving.

Purple rice

JAPGOKBAP

잡 곡 밥

SERVES 4

Preparation 5 minutes
Resting 55 minutes
Cooking 20 minutes

INGREDIENTS

160 g (5¾ oz) short-grain
  white rice
45 g (1½ oz) black rice
30 g (1 oz) quinoa
40 g (1½ oz) bulgar
40 g (1½ oz) green lentils
600 ml (2⅓ cups) water

Put the white rice, black rice, quinoa, bulgar and lentils in a bowl and cover with water (**A**). Mix lightly using your hand (**B–C**). Empty the water. Repeat the process twice. Once the rice is well drained, cover with the 600 ml (2⅓ cups) water (**D**). Leave to soak for 40 minutes (**E**).

Place the mixture in a Dutch oven, cover and heat over a high heat until boiling. When it first comes to the boil, open the lid for a few seconds to prevent it from overflowing and then close again (**F**). Repeat this process for the next three times it boils if it looks like the pan will overflow. After 10 minutes, reduce the heat to low, leaving it covered. Cook for 10 minutes, then turn off the heat. Stand for an additional 15 minutes, covered, before serving.

NOTE ——— *Rice mixed with other grains or legumes is known for its flavour but also for being easier to digest.*

RICE

Kimchi fried rice

KIMCHI BOKKEUMBAP

김치볶음밥

Like all Koreans, I will always have kimchi and cooked white rice in my refrigerator, making this fried rice the simplest and most popular dish to prepare at home.

SERVES 4
Preparation 15 minutes
Cooking 15 minutes

INGREDIENTS
400 g (14 oz) Chinese
  cabbage kimchi
  (page 90)
1 tablespoon sugar
1 teaspoon garlic powder
1 spring onion (scallion)
  stem (no bulb)
320 g (11¼ oz) tuna
  chunks in sunflower oil
2 tablespoons neutral
  vegetable oil
1 tablespoon gochugaru
  chilli powder
2 tablespoons soy sauce
1 tablespoon fermented
  anchovy sauce
400 g (14 oz) cooked
  white rice, cold (page 10)
4 eggs, fried

Place the kimchi in a bowl and use scissors to cut it into small pieces. Add the sugar and garlic powder and mix well. Stand for 5 minutes.

Chop the spring onion stem. Drain the tuna. Coat a frying pan with the vegetable oil. Tip in the chopped spring onion and turn the heat to high. Stir-fry until the spring onion starts to soften. Add the kimchi and gochugaru. Stir-fry for 5 minutes until the kimchi is a little translucent. Add the tuna, soy sauce and fermented anchovy sauce. Stir-fry for 5 minutes.

Add the cooked white rice to the frying pan when all the ingredients are well combined. Mix the rice through to obtain an even colour. When the rice has evenly taken on the colour of the kimchi, the cooking is complete.

Serve in individual portions by placing one fried egg on top of the kimchi bokkeumbap. Serve with soy sauce pickles (page 118) or white radish pickles (page 122) on the side, if desired.

TIP —— *You can sprinkle this dish with a few pieces of seaweed (gim or nori) and some chopped chives.*

RICE

Prawn and pineapple fried rice

HAWAIIAN BOKKEUMBAP

하 와 이 안 볶 음 밥

SERVES 4

Preparation 15 minutes
Cooking 20 minutes

INGREDIENTS

*½ spring onion (scallion)
  stem (no bulb)*
¼ cucumber
1 onion
1 carrot
½ pineapple
3 eggs
½ teaspoon salt
1 pinch pepper
1 teaspoon garlic powder
*40 g (1½ oz) butter, plus
  a knob*
*2 tablespoons mat
  ganjang sauce
  (page 146)*
*200 g (7 oz) peeled
  prawns*
*350 g (12 oz) cooked
  white rice, cold (page 10)*
Ketchup

Chop the spring onion stem. Cut the cucumber, onion and carrot into 5 mm (¼ inch) cubes. Cut the pineapple flesh into 1 cm (½ inch) cubes. Beat the eggs and season with the salt, pepper and garlic powder.

Heat the butter over a high heat in a frying pan. Add the spring onion and onion and stir-fry until the onion starts to become translucent. Add the carrot, cucumber and mat ganjang; cook until the carrot is tender. Add the pineapple and peeled prawns, then stir-fry for 3 minutes.

Add the cooked white rice to the frying pan. Mix evenly. Taste the seasoning and adjust with salt as needed. Push all the fried rice to one side of the frying pan. Place a knob of butter in the empty base of the pan. Add the beaten eggs and stir until they are half cooked – they should remain a little frothy. Mix through the rice.

Serve in the hollowed-out pineapple half or in individual portions with a few lines of ketchup drizzled on top. Serve with soy sauce pickles (page 118), white radish pickles (page 122) or marinated yellow radish on the side, if desired.

RICE

Vegetable, sausage and curry fried rice

CURRY BOKKEUMBAP

카레볶음밥

SERVES 4

Preparation 15 minutes
Cooking 25 minutes

INGREDIENTS

1 onion
2 medium potatoes
1 carrot
½ red capsicum (pepper)
½ zucchini (courgette)
4 knackwurst sausages
20 g (¾ oz) Korean (or Japanese) curry powder or paste
3 tablespoons water, plus 50 ml (scant ¼ cup)
30 g (1 oz) butter
50 g (1¾ oz) corn
350 g (12 oz) cooked white rice, cold (page 10)
Salt

Cut the onion, potatoes, carrot, capsicum and zucchini into 1 cm (½ inch) cubes. Cut the knackwurst sausages into 5 mm (¼ inch) thick slices. Dissolve the curry in the 3 tablespoons water.

Heat the butter over a high heat in a frying pan. Stir-fry the onion until it starts to become translucent. Add the corn and stir-fry for 3 minutes. Add the potato and carrot, then season with salt. Add the 50 ml (scant ¼ cup) water. Cook for about 10 minutes, until the potato and carrot are cooked. When the water has evaporated, add the zucchini, knackwurst and capsicum. Stir-fry for 5 minutes. Check the seasoning and add salt as needed.

When the zucchini is cooked, add the rice and curry. Mix well until the rice evenly takes on the colour of the curry.

Serve in individual portions with soy sauce pickles (page 118), white radish pickles (page 122) or kimchi, if desired.

RICE

Rice balls

JUMEOK-BAP

주 먹 밥

During school picnics with my friends, we used to make the most of the bus trip by sharing our rice balls. By lunchtime, we usually had already eaten everything!

SERVES 2

Preparation 15 minutes – Resting 5 minutes – Cooking 5 minutes

Tuna mayonnaise

INGREDIENTS

80 g (2¾ oz) tuna chunks in springwater, 50 g (1¾ oz) Chinese cabbage kimchi (page 90), ½ teaspoon sesame oil, ½ teaspoon sugar, ⅓ gim seaweed sheet (nori), 250 g (9 oz) cooked white rice, hot (page 10), 2 tablespoons mayonnaise, salt

Drain the tuna. Wash the kimchi and squeeze it with your hands to remove the juice, then chop finely. Mix the kimchi with the sesame oil and sugar. Cut the seaweed sheet into small pieces. Mix the tuna, seaweed and kimchi with the rice and season with salt and mayonnaise. Form balls the size of a ping-pong ball.

Surimi mayonnaise

INGREDIENTS

5 surimi (crab) sticks, ¼ onion, neutral vegetable oil, 5 cm (2 inch) piece cucumber, 250 g (9 oz) cooked white rice, hot (page 10), 3 tablespoons mayonnaise, salt

Chop the surimi. Chop the onion and sauté for 3 minutes in a little vegetable oil. Place the onion on paper towel to absorb the oil. Chop the cucumber, season with salt and stand for 5 minutes, then squeeze with your hands to remove any excess water. Mix all the ingredients with the rice and season with salt and mayonnaise. Form balls the size of a ping-pong ball.

Ham omelette

INGREDIENTS

1 slice leg ham, 1 egg, 1 pinch garlic powder, 1 tablespoon sesame seeds, 250 g (9 oz) cooked white rice, hot (page 10), 1 teaspoon sesame oil, salt

Chop the ham. Beat the egg and season with the garlic powder and salt. Scramble the egg, breaking into tiny pieces as you cook it. Crush the sesame seeds well. Mix all the ingredients with the rice and season with salt and the sesame oil. Form balls the size of a ping-pong ball.

RICE

Omelette, tuna and mayonnaise rice bowl

CHAMCHI-MAYO-DEOBPAB

참치마요덮밥

*I like to prepare this easy, fast and very satisfying recipe to eat when I'm short on time.
It is enjoyed while the rice is still hot.*

FOR 1 BOWL
Preparation 15 minutes
Cooking 3 minutes

INGREDIENTS
2 eggs
2 lettuce leaves
*¼ gim seaweed sheet
   (nori)*
*80 g (2¾ oz) tuna chunks
   in sunflower oil*
½ teaspoon sugar
1½ tablespoons soy sauce
*½ teaspoon gochugaru
   chilli powder*
½ teaspoon garlic powder
*180 g (6½ oz) cooked
   white rice, hot (page 10)*
2 tablespoons mayonnaise
Neutral vegetable oil
Salt and pepper

Beat the eggs well and season with salt and pepper. Heat a pan greased with vegetable oil. Pour in the eggs and stir to make scrambled eggs. Set aside.

Cut the lettuce leaves and seaweed sheet into thin strips. Drain the tuna, reserving a little of the oil. Mix the tuna and reserved oil in a bowl with the sugar, ½ tablespoon soy sauce, gochugaru and garlic powder.

Arrange the rice and then the lettuce in the serving bowl and drizzle with 1 tablespoon soy sauce. Add the scrambled eggs omelette, then the tuna. Drizzle generously with mayonnaise and finish by sprinkling with the gim seaweed.

Eat without mixing by trying to take a little of all the ingredients in a single bite.

RICE

Rice porridge

JUK

죽

Chicken

SERVES 4

Preparation 20 minutes – Resting 45 minutes
Cooking 1 hour 20 minutes

INGREDIENTS

150 g (5½ oz) short-grain white rice, 1.7 litres (7 cups)
water, 400 g (14 oz) chicken breast, 5 garlic cloves,
½ onion, 1 carrot, ½ zucchini (courgette), salt

Wash the rice three times. Soak for a minimum of
45 minutes in cold water.

Bring the 1.7 litres (7 cups) water to the boil in a pot.
Immerse the chicken breast and garlic cloves in the
water. Cook for 10 minutes, then reduce the heat to
medium. Cook for an additional 10 minutes. When
the chicken is well cooked, remove it from the broth
with a skimmer. Discard the garlic. When the chicken
has cooled, shred it into small pieces with your hands.

Chop the onion, carrot and zucchini. Drain the rice.

Pour 500 ml (2 cups) of the chicken broth into
a saucepan and add the rice. Bring to the boil.
Reduce the heat to medium, stirring regularly for
20 minutes. Add the vegetables. Add the remaining
broth gradually over the next 30 minutes over
a low heat, stirring regularly. Season with salt.

Beef

SERVES 4

Preparation 20 minutes – Resting 45 minutes
Cooking 1 hour

INGREDIENTS

150 g (5½ oz) short-grain white rice, 200 g (7 oz)
beef mince, ½ tablespoon fermented anchovy sauce,
½ tablespoon sugar, ½ teaspoon garlic powder,
1 teaspoon white alcohol (soju or gin), ½ onion,
1 carrot, 2 pyogo mushrooms (shiitake) or button
mushrooms, ½ zucchini (courgette), 1.2 litres (5 cups)
water, salt

Wash the rice three times. Soak for a minimum of
45 minutes in cold water.

Meanwhile, pat the beef with paper towel to
remove any excess blood. Mix the beef with the
anchovy sauce, sugar, garlic powder and alcohol.
Set aside for 20 minutes.

Chop the onion, carrot, mushrooms and zucchini.
Drain the rice.

Heat a saucepan. When it is hot, sauté the meat
for a few minutes, making sure to separate it
into small pieces with a spoon. Add the rice and
500 ml (2 cups) of the water. Bring to the boil.
Reduce the heat to medium, stirring regularly for
20 minutes. Add the vegetables. Add the remaining
water gradually over the next 30 minutes over
a low heat, stirring regularly. Season with salt.

NOTE ──── *To serve the porridge, beat 2 eggs and make a thin omelette. Leave to cool for a few minutes, then roll it up. Carefully cut the roll into sections without crushing it. Place a roll on the porridge in each bowl and season with a few drops of sesame oil. Arrange a few pine nuts and a jujube flower (page 196) on top.*

RICE

NOODLES, PANCAKES & FRITTERS

전과 튀김반죽

Korean noodles, tteokbokki tteok (rice cakes), fritters and pancakes are really delicious and come in a variety of flavours. When I cook them, the smell of the sauces and spluttering of oil takes me back to the street food stalls in Korea.

Tteokbokki tteok dough

TTEOKBOKKI TTEOK

떡볶이 떡

**MAKES AROUND 450 G
(1 LB) TTEOK**

*Preparation 20 minutes
Resting 40 minutes
Cooking 15 minutes*

INGREDIENTS

*160 g (5¾ oz) plain
    (all-purpose) flour
80 g (2¾ oz) glutinous
    rice flour
20 g (¾ oz) potato starch
1 teaspoon salt
About 170 ml (⅔ cup)
    water*

Sift the flours, starch and salt into a bowl. Stir in the 170 ml (⅔ cup) water gradually while kneading by hand until a smooth ball of dough is formed (**A**). Do not add more water when this consistency is obtained. Cover with a damp tea towel and stand for 10 minutes at room temperature.

Form a wide, even sausage (**B**). Cut it into 20 equal portions (**C**). Form smaller 1 cm (½ inch) thick logs with the pieces of dough (**D**) and cut each into two or three tteok (**E**). Even out the edges of each small piece if they have been slightly squashed during cutting to get an even thickness of 1 cm (½ inch).

Bring a saucepan of water to the boil and immerse the tteokbokki tteok. Stir gently, to prevent them from sticking to the bottom of the saucepan or to each other, until they rise to the surface. Cook for 10 minutes. Turn off the heat and leave to stand on the hob or hotplate for 3 minutes in the hot water. Quickly scoop up the tteokbokki tteok with a skimmer (**F**) and immerse them in a bowl of cold water. Remove them immediately and immerse them in a second bowl of cold water.

Take the tteokbokki tteok and arrange them one by one on a sheet of baking paper. Allow to dry for 30 minutes.

NOTE ——— *If you are not using the tteokbokki tteok immediately after making them, let them cool for twice as long and coat them with a thin layer of neutral vegetable oil so they do not stick together. They can be stored for 3 days in the refrigerator or several months in the freezer.*

NOODLES,
PANCAKES
& FRITTERS

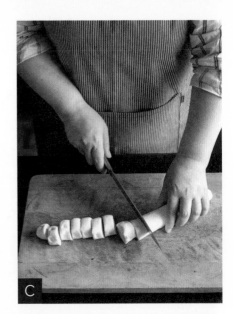

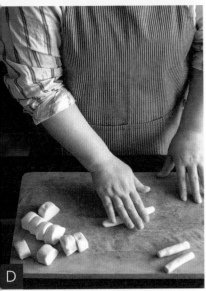

Stir-fried tteokbokki with chilli paste

TTEOKBOKKI

떡볶이

At the end of the school day, the smell of tteokbokki would always be wafting in the streets. This Korean street food speciality can be eaten at any time of the day and it was one of my favourite afternoon snacks.

SERVES 4
Preparation 10 minutes
Cooking 20 minutes

INGREDIENTS
4 eggs
2 spring onion (scallion)
    stems (no bulbs)
200 g (7 oz) fish paste
    (page 174)
500 ml (2 cups) water
1 vegetable stock cube
4 tablespoons sugar
300 g (10½ oz) tteokbokki
    tteok (page 26)
40 g (1½ oz) gochujang
    chilli paste
1 tablespoon gochugaru
    chilli powder
1 tablespoon soy sauce
½ tablespoon garlic
    powder

Hard boil the eggs. Cut the spring onions into 5 cm (2 inch) sections, then in half lengthways. Cut the fish paste diagonally into 1.2 cm (½ inch) thick sections.

Pour the water into a frying pan. Add the stock cube and sugar. Bring to the boil, then immediately reduce the heat to medium and tip in the tteokbokki tteok. Simmer for 5 minutes, stirring to prevent them from sticking to the bottom of the pan or to each other, separating them if necessary. Add the gochujang, gochugaru, soy sauce, garlic powder and fish paste.

Cook for 10 minutes, stirring regularly, before adding the peeled hard-boiled eggs and spring onion. The cooking is done when the tteokbokki tteok are soft and the sauce has reduced by half and coats the ingredients well.

NOTE —— *You can serve this dish with kimchi gimbap (page 116), sweet potato fritters (page 52) or seaweed vermicelli fritters (page 54), dipping them in the tteokbokki sauce. It can also be served with marinated yellow radish or white radish pickles (page 122) and lemonade (page 200) to temper the taste of the chilli while eating.*

NOODLES,
PANCAKES
& FRITTERS

Tteokbokki with black bean paste

JJAJANG-TTEOKBOKKI

짜 장 떡 볶 이

This dish is most often prepared in family kitchens. My mother often cooked it for me at afternoon tea time but you can enjoy it for lunch or dinner too.

SERVES 4

Preparation 20 minutes
Resting 20 minutes
Cooking 30 minutes

INGREDIENTS

300 g (10½ oz) tteokbokki
   tteok (page 26)
150 ml (generous ½ cup)
   water
3 tablespoons sugar
150 g (5½ oz) white
   cabbage
⅓ carrot
½ red onion
1 spring onion (scallion)
2 cm (¾ inch) leek
   (white part)
150 g (5½ oz) pork belly
150 g (5½ oz) fish paste
   (page 174)
2 tablespoons neutral
   vegetable oil
50 g (1¾ oz) unfried
   chunjang black bean
   paste
1 tablespoon soy sauce
1 tablespoon ginger syrup
   (page 202)

Stand the tteokbokki tteok in the water with the sugar for 20 minutes.

Cut the white cabbage into 5 cm (2 inch) long by 1 cm (½ inch) wide strips. Cut the carrot into matchsticks and the onion into thin strips. Cut the spring onion bulb into strips and the stem diagonally into 3 cm (1¼ inch) long sections and chop the leek. Cut the pork belly into small cubes. Cut the fish paste diagonally into 1 cm (½ inch) thick sections.

Heat the oil and chunjang paste in a frying pan over a high heat. Once it starts to boil, stir continuously for 5 minutes. Pour the fried chunjang into a fine mesh sieve over a bowl. Allow to drain for a few minutes to recover the oil. Pour the oil into a frying pan and add the leek. Heat over a low heat.

When the leek becomes aromatic, add the pork cubes, soy sauce and ginger syrup. Stir-fry for 3 minutes over a high heat. Add the remaining vegetables (except the spring onion stem), fish paste and chunjang. Stir while cooking for 5 minutes.

Add the tteokbokki tteok and soaking water to the frying pan. Allow to simmer for 10 to 15 minutes over a medium heat. Five minutes before the end of cooking, add the spring onion stem. Serve hot.

NOTE —— *To add a little extra bite to this recipe, you can add 1 teaspoon gochugaru chilli powder just before serving. Serve this dish with kimchi gimbap (page 116), sweet potato fritters (page 52) or seaweed vermicelli fritters (page 54).*

NOODLES,
PANCAKES
& FRITTERS

Tteokbokki with soy sauce

GANJANG-TTEOKBOKKI

간 장 떡 볶 이

SERVES 4

Preparation 10 minutes
Cooking 20 minutes

INGREDIENTS

⅔ carrot
10 cm (4 inch) leek
  (white part)
200 g (7 oz) fish paste
  (page 174)
250 ml (1 cup) water
3 tablespoons sugar
300 g (10½ oz) tteokbokki
  tteok (page 26)
100 ml (scant ½ cup)
  mat ganjang sauce
  (page 146)
½ teaspoon pepper
Sesame seeds

Cut the carrot in half into two logs, then each section in half lengthways and lastly into thin strips lengthways. Slice the leek diagonally into 2 cm (¾ inch) thick sections. Cut the fish paste diagonally.

Pour the water into a frying pan. Add the sugar and bring to the boil. Immediately reduce the heat to medium and tip in the tteokbokki tteok. Simmer for 5 minutes, stirring to prevent them from sticking to the bottom of the pan or to each other, separating them if necessary.

Add the mat ganjang, leek, carrot and fish paste. Simmer for 10 minutes, stirring constantly.

When the sauce has reduced by half, add the pepper and a generous pinch of sesame seeds. If necessary, add a little more mat ganjang.

NOTE —— *You can eat this dish served with hard-boiled eggs, sweet potato fritters (page 52) or seaweed vermicelli fritters (page 54) and white radish pickles (page 122).*

NOODLES,
PANCAKES
& FRITTERS

Tteok skewers with sweet-and-sour sauce

TTEOK-KKOCHI

떡 꼬 치

These skewers are an iconic Korean street food dish. Although they are slightly spicy, they are very popular with children who like the sweet-and-sour flavours.

FOR 6 SKEWERS

Preparation 20 minutes
Cooking 15 minutes

INGREDIENTS

36 tteokbokki tteok
  (page 26)
3 tablespoons ketchup
2 tablespoons sugar
1 teaspoon garlic powder
3 tablespoons soy sauce
½ tablespoon gochugaru
  chilli powder
15 g (½ oz) gochujang
  chilli paste
50 ml (scant ¼ cup) water
2 tablespoons corn syrup
Neutral vegetable oil

Bring a saucepan of water to the boil. Immerse the tteokbokki tteok in the boiling water for 3 minutes, then drain. When they have cooled slightly, thread them onto six wooden skewers (six tteok per skewer). If the tteokbokki tteok have just been made, skip this first step and prepare the skewers without letting them dry for 30 minutes (page 26).

Combine the ketchup, sugar, garlic powder, soy sauce, gochugaru, gochujang and the 50ml (scant ¼ cup) water in a saucepan. Bring to the boil and reduce the heat to low. Simmer for 5 minutes, stirring gently. Take off the heat and gradually stir in the corn syrup.

Pour vegetable oil into a frying pan up to half the height of a tteokbokki tteok. Heat and cook each skewer for 3 minutes on both sides.

Place the skewers on a tray and brush each side generously with the sauce using a pastry brush. Enjoy.

NOODLES,
PANCAKES
& FRITTERS

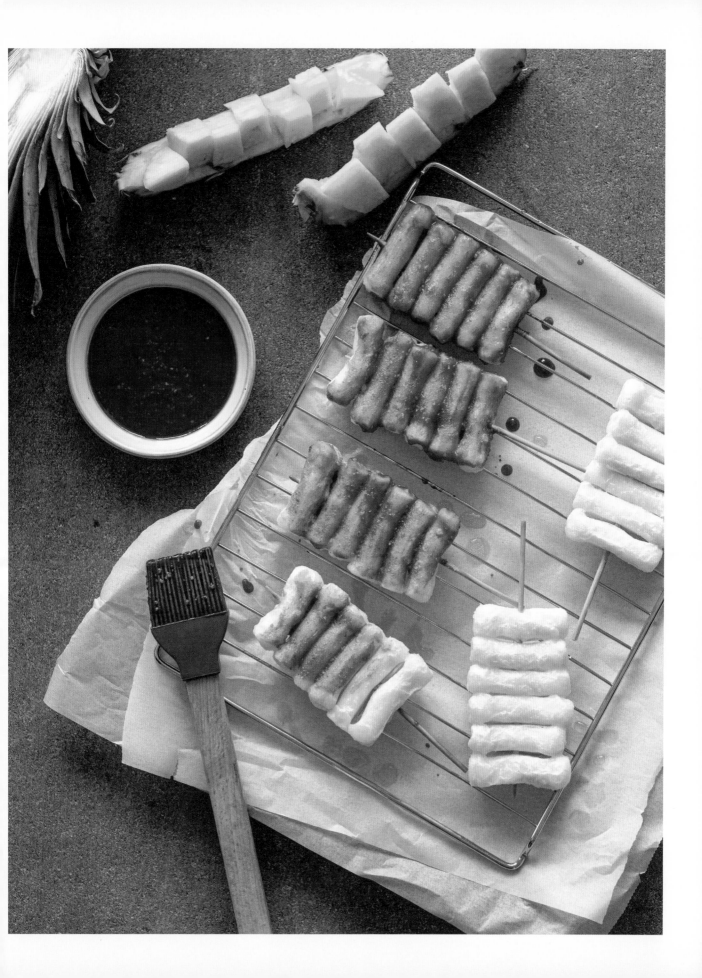

Korean pancake batter

JEON BANJUK

전 반 죽

MAKES 650 G (1 LB 7 OZ) BATTER
Preparation 10 minutes

INGREDIENTS
*250 g (9 oz) plain
   (all-purpose) flour
2 eggs
1 teaspoon salt
350 ml (scant 1½ cups)
   water*

Korean pancake sauce
*2 tablespoons soy sauce
1 tablespoon apple or
   apple cider vinegar
1 tablespoon sugar
1 pinch pepper
1 pinch sesame seeds*

Tip the flour into a bowl, add the eggs and salt.

Gradually stir in the water by mixing with a spatula. When the batter starts to become runny, continue to mix with a whisk. Whisk well to remove any lumps. The batter should have a crepe batter consistency: runny but still coating the back of a spoon.

Mix all the sauce ingredients together and serve with the pancakes.

NOTE ——— This batter can be used for many types of Korean pancakes.

Zucchini pancakes

HOBAKJEON

호박전

When I am feeling peckish between meals, I like to cook these tasty pancakes as a small snack to keep me going. Enjoy by yourself or share with others.

FOR 4 PANCAKES
Preparation 5 minutes
Cooking 30 minutes

INGREDIENTS
2 zucchini (courgettes)
½ carrot
½ onion
1 teaspoon garlic powder
1 pinch pepper
1 teaspoon salt
650 g (1 lb 7 oz) Korean
  pancake batter (page 36)
1 red chilli (optional)
Neutral vegetable oil

Grate the zucchini and carrot. Thinly slice the onion. Mix the vegetables, garlic powder, pepper, salt and batter. Deseed the chilli and finely dice (the chilli is optional or can be replaced with red capsicum/pepper).

Generously coat a frying pan with vegetable oil and heat over a high heat. Spread a thin layer of vegetable batter in the bottom of the pan. Sprinkle the diced red chilli evenly on the surface. Using a spatula, lift the batter from the bottom of the pan immediately to prevent it from sticking. As soon as the edges begin to brown and the surface sets slightly, turn the pancake over.

Cook the other side over a high heat for a further 4 minutes. Repeat for each pancake.

Enjoy with Korean pancake sauce (page 36) or onion soy sauce pickles (page 118).

NOODLES,
PANCAKES
& FRITTERS

Kimchi pancakes

KIMCHIJEON

김치전

When I invite my friends over, I cook this recipe for them to enjoy. All Koreans love kimchi and pancakes, so it's always a success!

FOR 4 PANCAKES

Preparation 15 minutes
Cooking 30 minutes

INGREDIENTS

*500 g (1 lb 2 oz) Chinese
cabbage kimchi (page 90)*
*2 teaspoons gochugaru
chilli powder*
*2 tablespoons fermented
anchovy sauce*
*650 g (1 lb 7 oz) Korean
pancake batter (page 36)*
Neutral vegetable oil

Cut the kimchi into small pieces with scissors and place in a bowl without draining the juice. Add the gochugaru chilli powder and fermented anchovy sauce. Add the pancake batter and mix well.

Generously coat a frying pan with vegetable oil and heat over a high heat. Spread a thin layer of kimchi batter in the bottom of the pan. Using a spatula, lift the batter from the bottom of the pan immediately to prevent it from sticking. As soon as the edges begin to brown and the surface sets slightly, turn the pancake over.

Cook the other side over a high heat for an additional 4 minutes. Repeat for each pancake.

Enjoy with Korean pancake sauce (page 36) or onion soy sauce pickles (page 118).

NOTE ——— *If you want to make a pork version, cut 200 g (7 oz) pork belly into small cubes and sauté them for 5 minutes in a frying pan. Fold the pork belly cubes through the batter just before cooking the pancakes.*

NOODLES,
PANCAKES
& FRITTERS

Seafood pancakes

HAEMUL-PAJEON

해 물 파 전

For Koreans, the sound of pancakes cooking is reminiscent of the sound of rain falling. On rainy days, I prepare these seafood pancakes at home to serve with a cup of makgeolli (Korean rice wine), just like I used to eat them in Korea.

FOR 4 PANCAKES

Preparation 20 minutes

Cooking 1 hour

INGREDIENTS

200 g (7 oz) squid

4 raw king prawns

60 g (2¼ oz) shucked mussels

60 g (2¼ oz) small scallops

200 g (7 oz) garlic chives

650 g (1 lb 7 oz) Korean pancake batter (page 36)

1 pinch pepper

Garlic powder

2 eggs

1 pinch salt

Neutral vegetable oil

Remove the squid innards, then cut the squid into strips. Peel the prawns using a small knife. Wash the mussels. If the scallops you are using are large, you can cut them into quarters. This recipe is suitable for both fresh and frozen seafood. Mix the seafood, except the king prawns, with the chives cut into 10 cm (4 inch) lengths, the pepper and garlic powder. Stir into the Korean pancake batter so that the ingredients are evenly distributed. Beat the eggs separately, seasoning them with the salt.

Generously coat a frying pan with vegetable oil. Heat over a high heat. When the oil is hot, cover the pan with a quarter of the seafood mixture. The layer of batter should be thinner than the thickness of a prawn. Place one prawn in the middle of the pancake and pour in a quarter of the beaten eggs, distributing them well over the entire surface without leaving any holes, then reduce the heat to medium. Using a spatula, lift the batter from the bottom of the pan immediately to prevent it from sticking.

After 5 to 7 minutes, when the edges of the pancake begin to brown, turn it over. Pour a thin drizzle of vegetable oil around the edge of the pancake, directly onto the metal of the pan. Cook for 5 to 7 minutes. Swich to a high heat for a final minute of cooking to give the pancake maximum crispiness. Repeat for the remaining pancakes.

Enjoy with Korean pancake sauce (page 36) or onion soy sauce pickles (page 118).

NOODLES,
PANCAKES
& FRITTERS

Tuna pancakes

CHAMCHI GYERAN-JEON

참치 계란전

This recipe is very popular with children in Korea but you can also choose the 'adults only' spicy version!

FOR 5 PANCAKES
Preparation 10 minutes
Cooking 20 minutes

INGREDIENTS
160 g (5¾ oz) tuna chunks
   in sunflower oil
½ carrot
¼ onion
½ green chilli (optional)
2 eggs
30 g (1 oz) plain
   (all-purpose) flour
½ teaspoon garlic powder
1 teaspoon salt
1 pinch pepper
Neutral vegetable oil

Lightly drain excess oil from the tin of tuna and place the tuna in a bowl. Chop the carrot and onion. For more spice, also chop the green chilli (making sure the seeds are removed and the inside has been rinsed with water). Mix the vegetables and tuna together. Combine the tuna and vegetable mixture with the eggs, flour, garlic powder, salt and pepper.

Heat vegetable oil in a large frying pan. When it is hot, pour in a ladle of batter and press to form a nice round pancake. Make several pancakes in the same pan. After 4 to 5 minutes, when the edges begin to brown, turn the pancakes over. Cook for 4 to 5 minutes on the other side. Switch to a high heat for a final minute of cooking to make the pancakes crispy. Both sides should be golden brown and have a slightly firm consistency.

Enjoy hot with ketchup or Korean pancake sauce (page 36).

NOODLES,
PANCAKES
& FRITTERS

Mung bean pancakes

NOKDU JEON

녹두전

I always remember making these pancakes with my mother for big family celebrations. Although the process is a little long, your efforts will be well rewarded as soon as you take the first bite.

FOR 6 PANCAKES
Preparation 40 minutes
Resting 12 hours
Cooking 50 minutes

INGREDIENTS
240 g (8½ oz) mung beans
100 g (3½ oz) pork belly
*1 tablespoon white
  alcohol (soju or gin)*
1 teaspoon garlic powder
*1 pinch salt, plus
  2 teaspoons*
1 pinch pepper
*200 g (7 oz) Chinese
  cabbage kimchi (page 90)*
100 g (3½ oz) bean sprouts
*1 spring onion (scallion)
  stem (no bulb)*
¼ red chilli
*Around 100 ml (scant
  ½ cup) water*
Neutral vegetable oil

Soak the mung beans in a large volume of cold water for 12 hours. When the soaking time is up, rub the beans vigorously between your hands to remove their skins (**A**). Pour the soaking water through a colander while keeping the beans in the bowl in order to get rid of some of the skins (**B**). Collect the water in a container and pour it over the beans (**C**). Continue this process until about 60% of the beans have no skin. Wash the beans well, drain and purée them completely in a small food processor (**D**).

Cut the pork belly into small cubes. Mix the cubes with the alcohol, garlic powder, 1 pinch of salt and pepper. Sauté in a hot pan for 5 minutes, then set aside.

Wash the kimchi lightly under running water, then squeeze with your hands to extract some of the juice. Cut it into small pieces.

Wash the bean sprouts. Cook them for 3 minutes in boiling water, uncovered. Using a colander, refresh them with cold water and then squeeze them in your hands to drain them.

Cut the spring onion into 1 cm (½ inch) sections. Cut the chilli into thin rounds.

In a bowl, mix the processed mung beans, kimchi, bean sprouts, pork cubes, spring onion, 2 teaspoons salt and around 100 ml (scant ½ cup) water (**E**). Adjust the amount of water if the batter is a bit too thick.

Heat vegetable oil in a large frying pan. When it is hot, pour in a ladleful of batter and press to form a nice round 1 cm (½ inch) thick pancake. Place one chilli round in the middle of the pancake. Make several pancakes in the same pan. After 10 minutes of cooking over a medium heat, when the underside has sufficiently set, turn the pancakes over (**F**). Turn the heat to high and cook the second side for 3 to 4 minutes.

Enjoy with Korean pancake sauce (page 36) or onion soy sauce pickles (page 118).

NOODLES,
PANCAKES
& FRITTERS

A

B

C

D

E

F

Korean fritter batter

TUIGIM BANJUK

튀김반죽

MAKES 600 G (1 LB 5 OZ) BATTER

Preparation 10 minutes

INGREDIENTS

Batter

300 g (10½ oz) plain
   (all-purpose) flour
1 egg
1 teaspoon salt
100 ml (scant ½ cup) beer
200 ml (generous ¾ cup)
   water

Tuigim sauce

2 tablespoons soy sauce
1 tablespoon apple
   or apple cider vinegar
1 pinch pepper

Place the flour, egg, salt and beer in a bowl. Stir in the water gradually while mixing. The batter should be smooth and free of lumps.

Mix all the sauce ingredients together. Serve the fritters with the sauce.

NOODLES,
PANCAKES
& FRITTERS

Sweet potato fritters

GOGUMA-TUIGIM

고구마튀김

SERVES 2
Preparation 10 minutes
Cooking 6 minutes
Resting 10 minutes

INGREDIENTS

1 large sweet potato
50 g (1¾ oz) plain
  (all-purpose) flour
½ teaspoon salt
1 litre (4 cups) neutral
  vegetable oil
300 g (10½ oz) Korean
  fritter batter (page 50)

Wash the sweet potato well and roughly peel it, leaving a few lines of skin. Cut it into 1 cm (½ inch) thick slices. Mix the flour and salt, then coat the slices of sweet potato. Make sure all the pieces are well coated with flour.

Heat the oil to 170°C (340°F). To check the temperature, let a drop of batter fall into the oil: if it immediately rises to the surface, the temperature is correct. Dip the sweet potato pieces into the fritter batter, then place them one at a time into the oil. Fry for around 4 minutes. The cooking is done when the fritters are golden brown.

Remove the fritters from the oil and drain in a colander for at least 5 minutes. Fry again in the oil for 2 minutes and allow to drain for another 5 minutes.

Serve hot, dipping in the tuigim sauce (page 50) or serving with stir-fried tteokbokki with chilli paste (page 28).

NOTE —— *You can store these fritters in the freezer and reheat them in the oven for 10 to 15 minutes at 200°C (400°F).*

NOODLES,
PANCAKES
& FRITTERS

Seaweed vermicelli fritters

GIMMARI
김말이

I like to eat these fritters with chilli tteokbokki, generously dipping them in the sauce to get a real explosion of flavours.

FOR 16 FRITTERS
Preparation 30 minutes
Resting 2 hours
Cooking 10 minutes

INGREDIENTS
100 g (3½ oz) sweet
   potato vermicelli
⅓ carrot
1 spring onion (scallion)
   stem (no bulb)
1 litre (4 cups) neutral
   vegetable oil, plus extra
   for the vegetables
2 tablespoons soy sauce
½ tablespoon sugar
½ tablespoon sesame oil
½ teaspoon pepper
1½ teaspoons salt
4 gim seaweed sheets
   (nori)
50 g (1¾ oz) plain
   (all-purpose) flour
300 g (10½ oz) Korean
   fritter batter (page 50)

Soak the vermicelli in cold water for 2 hours to separate.

Chop the carrot and spring onion. Sauté them for 3 minutes in a little vegetable oil. Cook the vermicelli in boiling water for 3 minutes. Using a colander, refresh them with cold water, then drain well. Place them in a bowl and cut with scissors twice, forming a cross shape. Mix with the sautéed vegetables, soy sauce, sugar, sesame oil, pepper and 1 teaspoon of salt.

Cut each gim seaweed sheet into four rectangles, cutting it lengthways then crosswise. Place one rectangle of seaweed on the worktop, rough side facing up. Arrange a little vermicelli mixture across the width, a little below the middle. Using cold water, moisten a 1.5 cm (⅝ inch) strip at the top of the sheet. Roll up tightly. The moistened part will stick and close the roll. Do the same for all the seaweed sheets.

Mix the flour with ½ teaspoon salt. Heat the oil to 170°C (340°F). To check the temperature, let a drop of batter fall into the oil: if it immediately rises to the surface, the temperature is correct. Lightly dust the seaweed rolls with the flour, ensuring they are evenly coated, then dip them in the fritter batter. Using tongs, dip each roll into the oil, moving it back and forth two or three times before releasing it into the oil.

Fry for around 4 minutes. The cooking is done when the fritters are golden brown. Remove the fritters from the oil and place in a colander to drain for at least 5 minutes. Fry in oil again for 2 minutes and allow to drain.

Serve hot, dipping in the tuigim sauce (page 50) or serving with stir-fried tteokbokki with chilli paste (page 28).

NOTE —— *You can store these fritters in the freezer and reheat them in the oven for 8 to 12 minutes at 200°C (400°F).*

NOODLES,
PANCAKES
& FRITTERS

Korean fried chicken

DAKGANGJEONG

닭 강 정

This recipe is the best reward after a long day of work. In the evening, I like to share this dish with my friends over a good beer.

SERVES 4

Preparation 15 minutes
Resting 20 minutes
Cooking 20 minutes

INGREDIENTS

700 g (1 lb 9 oz) chicken breasts, skin on
150 ml (generous ½ cup) milk
2 teaspoons salt
1 teaspoon mild paprika
1 teaspoon mild yellow curry powder
2 teaspoons garlic powder
600 g (1 lb 5 oz) Korean fritter batter
   (page 50)
1 litre (4 cups) neutral vegetable oil
3 crushed almonds (or peanuts)

Yangnyeom sauce

¼ apple
½ onion
3 garlic cloves
100 ml (scant ½ cup) water
5 tablespoons ketchup
20 g (¾ oz) gochujang chilli paste
1 tablespoon gochugaru chilli powder
4 tablespoons soy sauce
2 tablespoons sugar
5 tablespoons corn syrup
1 good pinch pepper

Cut the chicken breasts into roughly bite-sized pieces (**A**). Pour the milk over the chicken pieces (**B**). Cover and leave to rest for 20 minutes.

Drain the chicken using a colander. Place the chicken pieces in a bowl with the salt, paprika, curry and garlic powders. Massage the spices into the chicken. Mix with the fritter batter.

Heat the oil to 170°C (340°F). To check the temperature, let a drop of batter fall into the oil: if it immediately rises to the surface, the temperature is correct. Ensure each piece of chicken is well coated with batter and drop them into the oil (**C**). The chicken pieces should not stick to each other in the oil. Fry for around 5 minutes. Take the chicken out and let it drain for 5 minutes on a wire rack. Fry again for 3 minutes and allow to drain for 5 minutes.

For the yangnyeom sauce, purée the apple, onion and garlic in a small food processor. Combine with the water, ketchup, gochujang, gochugaru, soy sauce, sugar, corn syrup and pepper. Heat the mixture in a sauté pan or frying pan over a high heat. When the sauce simmers, just before boiling, reduce the heat. Mix very gently once or twice. Simmer for 7 minutes, stirring. Add the fried chicken and heat over a medium heat. Carefully coat the chicken with the sauce (**D**) then simmer for 2 minutes. Serve sprinkled with crushed almonds or peanuts (**E-F**).

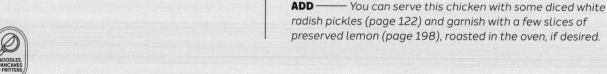

ADD ——— *You can serve this chicken with some diced white radish pickles (page 122) and garnish with a few slices of preserved lemon (page 198), roasted in the oven, if desired.*

NOODLES,
PANCAKES
& FRITTERS

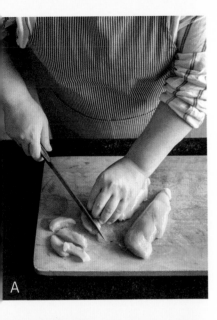

A

B

C

D

E

F

VEGETABLES
채 소

Korean tables are always dotted with several small
dishes, including salads, soups and sides to share.
In this chapter, you will discover the richness and
diversity of Korean recipes using vegetables.

Stir-fried white radish

MU-NAMUL
무나물

The word 'namul' means 'vegetable side dish' in Korean. This one was my grandfather's favourite dish and, as a result, my grandmother made sure that there was never a shortage at home.

SERVES 4
Preparation 10 minutes
Cooking 20 minutes

INGREDIENTS
450 g (1 lb) white radish
   (daikon)
2 cm (¾ inch) leek
   (white part)
2 garlic cloves
3 tablespoons sesame oil
1 tablespoon mat
   ganjang sauce
   (page 146)
1 teaspoon salt
1 teaspoon sugar
1 tablespoon sesame
   seeds

Peel the white radish and cut into 5 mm (¼ inch) thick matchsticks. Chop the leek white and crush the garlic.

Coat a frying pan with sesame oil and stir-fry the leek and garlic over a high heat until fragrant. Add the radish to the pan. Make a well in the middle of the radish sticks and pour in the mat ganjang. Allow to heat for 15 seconds, then mix well with the radish. After 4 minutes, stir in the salt and sugar and reduce the heat to medium. Stir-fry for around 15 minutes. If the radish starts to burn, add a little water.

The cooking is done when the radish is translucent and soft. Season with salt to taste. Serve sprinkled with sesame seeds. Enjoy hot or cold.

VEGETABLES

Stir-fried mushrooms

BEOSEOT-BOKKEUM

버섯볶음

*The type of mushroom used in this recipe is typically Korean. I am delighted to now
be able to find these mushrooms in Asian stores and sometimes even in supermarkets.*

SERVES 4

Preparation 5 minutes
Cooking 10 minutes

INGREDIENTS

5 saesongyi mushrooms
   (king oyster mushrooms)
2 cm (¾ inch) leek
   (white part)
2 tablespoons neutral
   vegetable oil
½ tablespoon sugar
1 tablespoon soy sauce
1 tablespoon oyster sauce
1 tablespoon honey
1 good pinch pepper
½ tablespoon black
   sesame seeds

Cut the mushrooms in half lengthways, then into long 5 mm (¼ inch) thick strips. Chop the leek.

Coat a frying pan with the vegetable oil and stir-fry the leek over a high heat until fragrant. Add the mushrooms to the pan and stir-fry. When the juice of the mushrooms starts to come out, make a well in the middle of the pan, and pour in the sugar, soy and oyster sauces. Allow to heat for 15 seconds, then mix well with the mushrooms. Stir-fry for a further 2 minutes.

Turn off the heat but leave the pan on the hob or hotplate. Season with the honey and pepper, then mix together. Serve sprinkled with sesame seeds. Enjoy hot or cold.

VEGETABLES

Stir-fried green beans

GREEN BEANS BOKKEUM

그린빈 볶음

I created this recipe since moving to live in France. It combines Korean and French flavours. My French husband loves it.

SERVES 4
Preparation 15 minutes
Cooking 15 minutes

INGREDIENTS
500 g (1 lb 2 oz) thin
   green beans
10 garlic cloves
100 g (3½ oz) smoked
   bacon
2 tablespoons sesame
   seeds
3 tablespoons olive oil
2 tablespoons mat
   ganjang sauce
   (page 146)
1 teaspoon salt

Top and tail and wash the green beans. Bring some salted water to the boil in a saucepan and tip in the beans. Cook for 2 minutes after it comes to the boil. Drain the beans immediately and refresh them under cold water. Peel the garlic cloves, cut them in half and remove the germ, if desired. Cut the bacon into 1 cm (½ inch) wide pieces. Crush the sesame seeds well.

Coat the base of a frying pan with the olive oil and stir-fry the garlic over a high heat until golden. Add the bacon to the pan and stir-fry. When the bacon is cooked, add the beans and mat ganjang. Stir-fry for 5 minutes. Add the crushed sesame seeds and season with the salt. Stir-fry for a further 2 minutes. Enjoy hot or cold.

VEGETABLES

Stir-fried zucchini

HOBAK-NAMUL

호박나물

When I prepare 'namul', vegetable side dishes, I always cook several types at the same time. On the first day, I eat them with a bowl of rice, and the following day, I like to use them to garnish a bibimbap.

SERVES 4
Preparation 10 minutes
Cooking 10 minutes

INGREDIENTS
2 zucchini (courgettes)
½ onion
½ carrot
2 garlic cloves
2 tablespoons neutral vegetable oil
2 teaspoons fermented anchovy sauce
1 teaspoon sesame oil
½ teaspoon sesame seeds
Salt

Cut the zucchini in half lengthways, then into 5 mm (¼ inch) thick half moons. Thinly slice the onion and cut the carrot into matchsticks. Crush the garlic.

Coat the base of a frying pan with the vegetable oil and stir-fry the garlic over a high heat until fragrant. Add the onion and carrot. Stir-fry until the onion starts to become translucent. Add the zucchini and fermented anchovy sauce. Stir-fry for 3 to 5 minutes. The zucchini should remain slightly crunchy. Taste and add salt to taste.

Off the heat, add the sesame oil and sesame seeds. Mix together gently in the pan while still hot. Enjoy hot or cold.

Sesame spinach

SIGEUMCHI-NAMUL

시금치나물

SERVES 4

Preparation 10 minutes
Cooking 5 minutes

INGREDIENTS

2 garlic cloves
1 cm (½ inch) leek (white part)
600 g (1 lb 5 oz) fresh spinach
½ tablespoon mat ganjang
* sauce (page 146)*
3 tablespoons sesame oil
½ tablespoon sesame seeds
Salt

Crush the garlic cloves and finely chop the leek. Clean the spinach leaves, cutting the stems if they are too thick. If the leaves are very wide, cut them in half crosswise.

Bring salted water to the boil in a saucepan and tip in the spinach. As soon as the leaves begin to wilt, drain them in a colander and run them under cold water to stop them cooking. Take large handfuls of the cooled leaves and squeeze them with your hands to remove excess water, then place in a bowl.

Add the garlic, leek, mat ganjang and sesame oil to the spinach. Rub the sesame seeds vigorously between your hands to crush them, then add them to the spinach mixture. Carefully mix it all together, unsticking the spinach leaves. Check the seasoning and adjust salt to taste.

Sesame bean sprouts

SUKJU-NAMUL

숙주나물

SERVES 4

Preparation 10 minutes
Cooking 5 minutes

INGREDIENTS

2 garlic cloves
½ carrot
1 cm (½ inch) leek (white part)
500 g (1 lb 2 oz) bean sprouts
3 tablespoons sesame oil
½ tablespoon sesame seeds
Salt

Crush the garlic, grate the carrot and chop the leek. Wash the bean sprouts, taking care not to break them.

Bring salted water to the boil in a saucepan and immerse the bean sprouts in the water. Cook, uncovered, for 4 minutes. Using a colander, run the bean sprouts under cold water to stop them cooking. Take large handfuls of cooled bean sprouts and squeeze them with your hands to remove excess water, taking care not to crush them too much. Place them in a bowl.

Add the garlic, carrot and leek to the bean sprouts. Season with sesame oil and salt. Rub the sesame seeds vigorously between your hands to crush them, then add them to the vegetable mixture and carefully mix it all together.

VEGETABLES

Spicy white radish salad

MU-SAENGCHAE

무 생 채

I like the subtle balance between the sweet, acidic and spicy flavours of this salad. I often eat it with rice, a fried egg, a dash of sesame oil and a touch of gochujang chilli paste, and I mix it all together like a small bibimbap.

SERVES 4

Preparation 15 minutes
Resting 40 minutes

INGREDIENTS

450 g (1 lb) white radish
   (daikon)
½ tablespoon salt
3 tablespoons sugar
1 spring onion (scallion)
   stem (no bulb)
3 garlic cloves
15 g (½ oz) gochugaru
   chilli powder
4 tablespoons apple or
   apple cider vinegar
1 tablespoon fermented
   anchovy sauce
1 teaspoon sesame seeds
½ teaspoon ground ginger
Salt

Cut the white radish into matchsticks. Mix the radish with the salt and sugar, stand for 10 minutes, then drain the juice. Cut the spring onion into 5 mm (¼ inch) sections and crush the garlic.

After the 10 minutes standing time, combine all the vegetables in the bowl containing the drained white radish. Add the gochugaru, vinegar, anchovy sauce, sesame seeds and ground ginger. Mix well and stand for a minimum of 30 minutes so that the radish takes on the flavours of the seasoning.

Serve chilled, adjusting the seasoning with a little salt as needed.

VEGETABLES

Homemade bibimbap

BIBIMBAP

비빔밥

The translation of 'bibimbap' is literally 'mixed rice'. It is, above all, a home-cooked dish that allows you to use up the week's leftover cooked vegetables.

FOR 1 BOWL
Preparation 10 minutes
Cooking 3 minutes

INGREDIENTS
1 tablespoon neutral vegetable oil
1 egg
1 bowl cooked white rice, hot (page 10)
1 handful stir-fried white radish (page 60)
1 handful sesame spinach (page 68)
1 handful spicy white radish salad (page 70)
1 handful sesame bean sprouts (page 68)
1 handful stir-fried mushrooms (page 62)
1 handful stir-fried zucchini (page 66)
Pine nuts or sesame seeds

Sauce
20 g (¾ oz) gochujang chilli paste
1 tablespoon sesame oil

Coat a 9 cm (3½ inch) diameter frying pan with the vegetable oil. Heat the oil over a medium heat. Break the egg into the pan. Using a spoon, gently move the yolk of the egg so that it remains in the middle. Hold the egg yolk like this until it sets. Reduce the heat to low and fry until the egg white is cooked.

Tip a bowl of hot rice into the bottom of the serving bowl. Place the egg on top of the rice dome with the yolk nicely in the middle. Arrange the stir-fried white radish, sesame spinach, spicy white radish salad, sesame bean sprouts, stir-fried mushrooms and stir-fried zucchini around the egg. The same colour ingredients should not touch each other. Sprinkle a few pine nuts or sesame seeds on top.

Mix together the sauce ingredients and drizzle directly into the serving bowl. For a less spicy version, replace the gochujang with soy sauce.

To eat the bibimbap, mix all the ingredients with a spoon, cutting the egg into pieces. The ingredients and sauce must be evenly distributed.

NOTE ——— *For a meat version, you can, for example, add leftover beef bulgogi ssambap (page 150) or pork bulgogi (page 134).*

VEGETABLES

Seasonings
FERMENTED SOYBEAN PASTE AND CHILLI PASTE

AN ANCESTRAL PRACTICE

The tradition of preparing fermented soybean paste goes back to the dawn of time. The first written records about its manufacture date to over 1800 years ago but many agree that it could be much older. From this ancestral practice, two treasures of Korean cuisine were born: **doenjang soybean paste** and **gochujang chilli paste**. Traditionally, it was customary to call on a shaman to determine the precise date on which to begin preparation – sometime between autumn and the beginning of winter. Various superstitions and rituals were also common to prevent evil spirits from entering and spoiling the preparation.

TRADITIONAL PREPARATION

The process starts with drying the soybeans. Once dry, they are boiled and ground. Blocks called 'meju' are then made from the paste obtained. These blocks are dried and covered with rice plants. It is these rice plants, and more specifically the good bacteria they contain, that start the slow fermentation process essential for preservation. This process can take up to 3 months. The second stage of fermentation follows, this time by immersing the blocks of meju in brine in airtight jars. This is when the special flavours develop and seasoning is added. The pure version results in two ingredients: firstly **doenjang**, fermented soybean paste, and also a particularly subtle light soy sauce called 'joseon ganjang'. The addition of chilli and various other ingredients to the remaining meju brine becomes **gochujang** – Korean fermented chilli paste.

READY-TO-USE PRODUCTS

The complexity of these preparations means that it is no longer customary to make them at home, even though there are still some traditional manufacturers in Korea. These products are available in Asian grocery stores and online. Their fermentation allows them to be kept for several months in the refrigerator after opening without going bad.

Sweet-and-sour lotus roots

YEONGEUN-JORIM
연근조림

I like the crunchy texture of lotus roots in this recipe, which they retain even once they are cooked. The sweet-and-sour combination of the sauce together with the flavour of this plant is unique.

SERVES 4
Preparation 10 minutes
Resting 20 minutes
Cooking 50 minutes

INGREDIENTS
500 ml (2 cups) water
1 square (10 cm/4 inches)
   dasima seaweed (kombu)
500 g (1 lb 2 oz) lotus
   roots
1 tablespoon white
   vinegar
4 tablespoons sugar
2 tablespoons neutral
   vegetable oil
100 ml (scant ½ cup) soy
   sauce
2 tablespoons white wine
1 tablespoon honey
½ tablespoon sesame
   seeds

Pour the 500 ml (2 cups) water into a saucepan and add the dasima seaweed. Bring to the boil and cook for 20 minutes over a medium heat. Discard the seaweed and keep the broth.

Peel the lotus roots and cut them into 1 cm (½ inch) thick slices. Place them in a saucepan and cover with cold water. Add the vinegar. Bring to the boil over a high heat and cook for 10 minutes. Drain and rinse the lotus roots under cold water. Discard the cooking water.

Mix the lotus roots and sugar in a bowl. Allow to stand at room temperature until the sugar has dissolved.

Heat a frying pan coated with the vegetable oil. When the oil is slightly hot, pour in the lotus roots with their sweet liquid. Pour the soy sauce, white wine and seaweed broth on top. Simmer over a medium heat until no liquid remains, about 20 to 30 minutes. Turn off the heat and add the honey and sesame seeds.

This side dish can be enjoyed warm or cold and can be kept for up to 5 days in the refrigerator.

NOTE —— *Instead of dasima seaweed broth, you can use 400 ml (1½ cups) water, and 120 ml (½ cup) mat ganjang sauce (page 146) instead of the soy sauce.*

VEGETABLES

Tofu salad

DUBU-SALAD

두부샐러드

This light salad is the perfect side to serve with Korean appetisers. It is called an
'anju', a dish to share with a drink.

SERVES 2
Preparation 10 minutes
Cooking 15 minutes

INGREDIENTS
300 g (10½ oz) firm tofu
3 tablespoons neutral
   vegetable oil
½ yellow capsicum
   (pepper)
20 cherry tomatoes
¼ red oak leaf lettuce
300 g (10½ oz) lamb's
   lettuce
Black sesame seeds
Salt

Sauce
½ lemon
4 tablespoons mat
   ganjang sauce
   (page 146)
2 tablespoons olive oil
½ teaspoon pepper
½ shallot

Cut the block of tofu into 1.5 cm (⅝ inch) cubes. Heat a frying pan coated with the vegetable oil and place the tofu cubes into the pan. Fry over a medium heat until all the sides are golden, using a spatula and a spoon to turn the cubes so as not to break them. Season each side with salt while cooking. After cooking, let the tofu cool on some paper towel.

Cut the capsicum into thin strips. Cut the cherry tomatoes in half.

For the sauce, squeeze the lemon and mix the juice with the mat ganjang, olive oil and pepper. Chop the shallot and add it to the sauce.

Arrange the oak leaf and lamb's lettuces in a serving dish. Scatter the tofu, capsicum and cherry tomatoes on top. Sprinkle with sesame seeds and drizzle with the sauce.

VEGETABLES

Surimi salad

KEURAEMI-SALAD

크래미 샐러드

SERVES 4
Preparation 10 minutes
Resting 10 minutes

INGREDIENTS
¼ green lettuce
¼ onion
⅓ cucumber
1 tablespoon sesame
   seeds
12 surimi (crab) sticks

Sauce
2 teaspoons apple or
   apple cider vinegar
2 tablespoons sugar
1 tablespoon soy sauce
1 teaspoon mustard
½ teaspoon pepper

Wash the lettuce, then drain and tear the leaves. Thinly slice the onion and soak in a bowl of water with a few drops of vinegar. Allow to stand in the water for 10 minutes, then drain. Cut the cucumber into matchsticks. Crush the sesame seeds well. Shred the surimi sticks into strips using your hands.

Mix all the sauce ingredients together to make the sauce.

Just before serving, arrange the lettuce in a bowl. Toss everything together, including the sauce and sesame seeds.

VEGETABLES

Sesame potato stir-fry

GAMJACHAE-BOKKEUM

감 자 채 볶 음

This potato side dish is one of my favourites. It goes very well with many Korean dishes, such as seasoned gim seaweed sheets (nori), or even with a simple bowl of white rice.

SERVES 4

Preparation 15 minutes
Cooking 20 minutes

INGREDIENTS

6 medium potatoes
½ carrot
½ onion
2 tablespoons neutral
   vegetable oil
1 teaspoon salt
1 pinch pepper
1 handful sesame seeds

Peel the potatoes and cut them into very thin matchsticks. Cut the carrot the same way and thinly slice the onion.

Heat a frying pan generously coated with vegetable oil. Add the potatoes and season with the salt. Stir-fry for 5 minutes to coat the potatoes with the oil. Add the onion and carrot. Stir-fry for 10 to 15 minutes, making sure that it does not burn and regularly adding a little water.

When the vegetables are cooked but still slightly crunchy, turn off the heat. Adjust the salt level if necessary and add the pepper. Rub the sesame seeds vigorously between your hands to crush them and then add them to the mixture.

Serve as a hot or cold side dish.

VEGETABLES

Iced seaweed soup

MIYEOK-NAENGGUK

미 역 냉 국

A fresh soup recipe ideal for hot days in Korea – or anywhere.

SERVES 4
Preparation 15 minutes
Resting 20 minutes

INGREDIENTS
10 g (¼ oz) miyeok
   seaweed (wakame)
100 g (3½ oz) white
   radish (daikon)
½ tablespoon salt
5 tablespoons sugar
½ carrot
¼ onion
100 ml (scant ½ cup)
   apple or white vinegar
1 teaspoon fermented
   anchovy sauce
2 tablespoons mat
   ganjang sauce
   (page 146)
600 ml (2⅓ cups) mineral
   water
1 pinch sesame seeds
Ice cubes, to serve

Allow the seaweed to rehydrate for 20 minutes in a large bowl filled with water. Drain and pour 1 litre (4 cups) boiling water over the seaweed before cooling it under running water and then draining again. Squeeze the seaweed with your hands to remove excess water and roughly cut it using scissors.

Cut the radish into matchsticks. Marinate with the salt and 1 tablespoon of the sugar for 15 minutes. Drain and press lightly with your hands to extract some of the liquid. Cut the carrot into matchsticks. Cut the onion into matchsticks and stand for 10 minutes in cold water with a few drops of vinegar, then drain.

Mix the seaweed, vinegar and 4 tablespoons of the sugar together in a bowl. Add the onion, carrot, radish, fermented anchovy sauce, mat ganjang and mineral water. Mix again and season with salt.

Before serving, sprinkle with the sesame seeds and add a few ice cubes to the serving bowl.

NOTE ——— *Summer in Korea is long and hot. Since Korean meals usually include at least one soup, this type of very cold dish helps people get through the hot days. Serve this soup with a rice porridge (page 22) or a homemade bibimbap (page 72).*

VEGETABLES

Stuffed capsicums

PEPPER GYERAN-JJIM

파프리카 계란찜

This very simple recipe is a reworked version of a traditional dish that was inspired by a famous Korean actor. I really like both versions.

FOR 3 CAPSICUMS

Preparation 10 minutes
Cooking 30 minutes

INGREDIENTS

3 medium capsicums
  (peppers)
⅓ carrot
5 chive stems
6 eggs
1 teaspoon garlic powder
Salt and pepper
Grated cheese (optional)

Preheat the oven to 200°C (400°F).

Cut the tops off the capsicums and hollow them out without piercing to make three bowls.

Chop the carrot and chives. Mix with the beaten eggs, garlic powder and a good amount of salt and pepper.

Fill the capsicums with the egg mixture up to 5 mm (¼ inch) from the top. You can fill the remaining space with a generous handful of grated cheese, if desired.

Put the stuffed capsicums and tops on a baking tray. Place a small ramekin filled with water next to the capsicums to prevent them from drying out during cooking, and bake for 30 minutes.

VEGETABLES

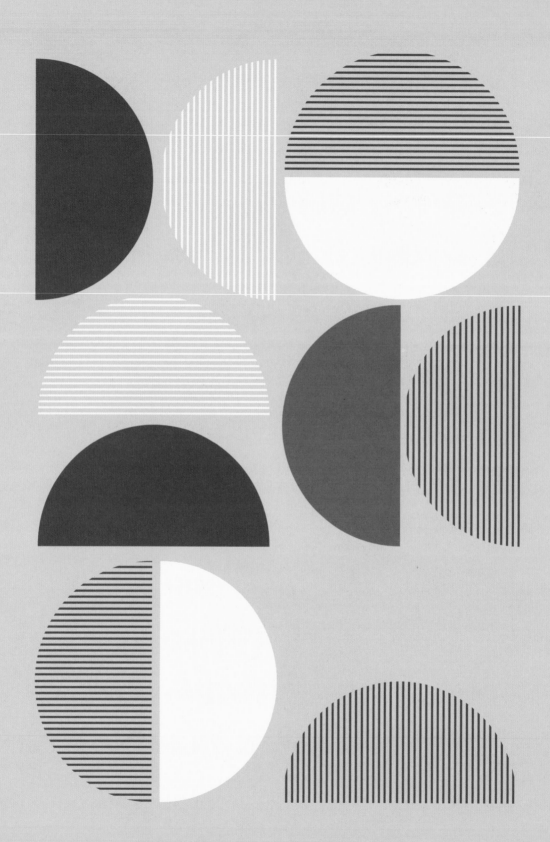

KIMCHI & PICKLES

김치와 장아찌

Kimchi is much more than just a recipe: it is an art of living and a tradition shared by all Korean families. Learn how to ferment your own vegetables, following the process step-by-step, and discover the wonderful power of kimchi in your everyday cooking.

Chinese cabbage kimchi

BAECHU-KIMCHI

배 추 김 치

**MAKES AROUND 3 KG
(6 LB 12 OZ)**

*Preparation 1¼ hours
Resting 4 to 6 hours
+ 24 hours
Cooking 10 minutes*

INGREDIENTS

Brine

2 Chinese cabbages,
   approximately 1.8 kg
   (4 lb) each
350 g (12 oz) coarse sea
   salt
2 litres (8 cups) water

Marinade

300 ml (1¼ cups) water
15 g (½ oz) rice flour
100 g (3½ oz) gochugaru
   chilli powder
10 g (¼ oz) ginger
1 small onion
1 pear
70 g (2½ oz) fermented
   anchovy sauce
50 g (1¾ oz) sugar
80 g (2¾ oz) garlic,
   crushed
1 bunch spring onions
   (scallions)
400 g (14 oz) white radish
   (daikon)
Sea salt

Gently cut and discard the hard end of the cabbages, ensuring the leaves remain attached together. Cut the Chinese cabbages into quarters. To do this, use a long, very sharp knife. Starting from the base, cut each cabbage two-thirds of the way to the top. Separate the two parts by hand (**A**), tearing the top of the leaves. Do the same for the two halves to obtain quarters of cabbage. Dilute 200 g (7 oz) of the coarse sea salt in the 2 litres (8 cups) water, stirring vigorously to make the brine. Dip each cabbage quarter in the brine, ensuring they are well moistened. Distribute one handful of the remaining salt between the leaves around the firm base section of each cabbage quarter.

Place the cabbage quarters in a container with the remaining brine and with the inside of the leaves facing upwards. Leave for 3 to 5 hours, checking the elasticity of the leaves near the end. If the hard base of the leaves bends between two fingers without breaking, the brining is done. Rinse the cabbage three times in a row, then leave to drain for a minimum of 1 hour.

Prepare the rice flour soup (**B**). Pour 300 ml (1¼ cups) water and the rice flour into a saucepan. Stir and bring to the boil, stirring regularly, then lower the heat while continuing to stir for about 10 minutes. Allow to cool, then mix with the gochugaru chilli powder (**C**).

Purée the ginger, onion and half the pear in a small food processor. Stir this mixture into the rice flour mixture. Add the anchovy sauce (**D**), sugar, crushed garlic and spring onions that have been cut in four widthways and in two lengthways. Cut the white radish and remaining half pear into matchsticks and add to the mixture. Finish the seasoning with sea salt as needed.

Brush each cabbage quarter with the marinade (**E**), including between the leaves. Position each cabbage quarter with the outer leaves facing downwards in an airtight container (**F**). Fill only to 70% full. Cover any solitary cabbage leaves with the marinade, cover with plastic wrap and close tightly with the lid. Leave for 24 hours in the dark at room temperature and then store in the refrigerator for up to 6 months.

NOTE ——— *Kimchi can be consumed 'fresh' the first 10 days after its preparation. Fermentation starts from about 3 weeks. If you want to consume it fresh as well as ferment it, keep a small amount in a separate container.*

KIMCHI
& PICKLES

Cucumber kimchi

OI-SOBAGI

오 이 소 박 이

I usually prepare this kimchi to celebrate the arrival of spring. This recipe perfectly embodies all the pretty colours of nature and scents as buds reappear after winter.

MAKES AROUND 1.5 KG (3 LB 5 OZ)

Preparation 50 minutes
Resting 5 to 8 hours
+ 24 hours

INGREDIENTS

Brine
15 baby cucumbers
   (1.5 kg/3 lb 5 oz)
100 g (3½ oz) coarse
   sea salt, plus extra for
   cleaning the cucumbers
1 litre (4 cups) water

Marinade
60 g (2¼ oz) rice flour
   soup (page 90)
80 g (2¾ oz) chives
2 spring onions (scallions)
50 g (1¾ oz) garlic cloves
50 g (1¾ oz) gochugaru
   chilli powder
50 g (1¾ oz) fermented
   anchovy sauce
Sea salt

Prepare the baby cucumbers: cut 5 mm (¼ inch) off the ends and wash under cold water, rubbing them with coarse salt to remove impurities from the skin. Place in a large bowl. Mix the coarse sea salt with the 1 litre (4 cups) water until the salt dissolves, then pour over the cucumbers. Stand for 5 to 8 hours, flipping the cucumbers from top to bottom every 90 minutes. To check if the brining is done, gently fold a cucumber. It must be supple and bend without breaking. Wash the cucumbers twice with clean water and pat dry.

Prepare the marinade by placing the rice flour soup in a bowl. Wash and cut the chives into 1 cm (½ inch) pieces. Cut the spring onion bulbs into matchsticks and the stems in half lengthways, then into 1 cm (½ inch) pieces. Crush the garlic. Mix the vegetables with the rice flour soup and add the gochugaru and fermented anchovy sauce. Finish seasoning with sea salt, if neeeded.

Cut the cucumbers. To do this, place each cucumber on a board and cut into two sections by placing the tip of the knife 1 cm (½ inch) from the end and gently making a cut. When the knife blade touches the board, grab the cucumber, turn and move it up the blade to separate well. Do the same on the second side so that the cucumbers are cut into four sticks still attached to the base. Fill each cucumber with 1 or 2 pinches of marinade. Rub the marinade into the outside of the cucumbers as well.

Fill an airtight container to 70% full with the cucumbers, placing them nicely flat and making several layers. Cover with plastic wrap and close the lid tightly. Leave at room temperature for 24 hours away from sunlight, then store in the refrigerator. This kimchi can be eaten fresh or fermented from the next day. The cucumbers will remain crunchy for about 2 months.

KIMCHI & PICKLES

White radish kimchi

KKAKDUGI

깍 두 기

*I like to prepare this white radish kimchi when I feel the first chill of winter.
It goes perfectly with comforting soup recipes.*

**MAKES AROUND 1.6 KG
(3 LB 8 OZ)**
*Preparation 40 minutes
Resting 4½ hours
+ 24 hours*

INGREDIENTS

Brine
1.5 kg (3 lb 5 oz) peeled
   white radish (daikon),
   black radish or turnip
40 g (1½ oz) coarse sea
   salt
50 g (1¾ oz) sugar
250 ml (1 cup) sparkling
   water

Marinade
60 g (2¼ oz) gochugaru
   chilli powder
110 g (3¾ oz) plain
   (all-purpose) flour soup
   (page 90)
½ pear
½ onion
50 g (1¾ oz) fermented
   anchovy sauce
60 g (2¼ oz) garlic cloves
1 teaspoon ground ginger
5 cm (2 inches) leek
   (white part)
½ tablespoon sea salt
2 tablespoons sugar

Cut the radish into 1.2 cm (½ inch) thick sections, then each section into quarters. Place them in a bowl and add the coarse sea salt, sugar and sparkling water. Mix well using your hands so that the sugar and salt are well rubbed in. Stand for around 4 hours at room temperature. When the radish pieces become elastic, the brining is done. Rinse the radish pieces once in water. Let them drain for a minimum of 30 minutes.

For the marinade, mix the gochugaru into the cold plain flour soup (same preparation technique as for the rice flour soup, page 90). Purée the pear, onion and fermented anchovy sauce in a small food processor and mix with the gochugaru plain flour mixture. Crush the garlic and stir it into the mixture along with the ground ginger. Cut the leek into thin slices and stir into the mixture. Finish the seasoning with the sea salt and sugar.

Combine the radish pieces with the marinade. Place in an airtight container, filling it to 70% full. Cover with plastic wrap and press to remove as much air as possible. Close the lid tightly. Leave for 24 hours in the dark at room temperature and then store in the refrigerator for up to 6 months. The taste of this kimchi is at its best when it is well fermented, which is after around 3 weeks.

KIMCHI
& PICKLES

Chive kimchi

PA-KIMCHI

파 김 치

When I miss Korea a little too much, I make this kimchi, which brings back the flavours of home. This is probably one of the easiest kimchi to prepare.

MAKES AROUND 500 G (1 LB 2 OZ)

Preparation 45 minutes
Resting 30 minutes
+ 24 hours

INGREDIENTS

Brine
400 g (14 oz) garlic chives
50 g (1¾ oz) fermented
   anchovy sauce

Marinade
40 g (1½ oz) gochugaru
   chilli powder
30 g (1 oz) rice flour soup
   (page 90)
¼ pear
¼ onion
25 g (1 oz) garlic cloves
1 tablespoon preserved
   lemon (page 198)
½ teaspoon ground ginger
1 tablespoon sugar

Wash the chive stalks well and remove the roots. Arrange the bunch of chives, bulbs facing down, in a large bowl. Pour the anchovy sauce over the chives, directly onto the lowest part. All the stems should be well moistened. Help spread the sauce with your hands, smoothing from bottom to top. Every 10 minutes, move the sauce in the same way from the bottom of the bowl to the top of the stems, and continue doing this for 30 minutes.

Stir the chilli powder into the rice flour soup. Purée the pear and onion together in a small food processor and crush the garlic. Mix with the rice flour soup. Pour the mixture into the bowl containing the chives. Add the preserved lemon, ground ginger and sugar. Mix by coating each chive stalk with the marinade.

Place in an airtight container, filling to 70% full. Cover with plastic wrap and press to remove as much air as possible. Close the lid tightly. Leave for 24 hours in the dark at room temperature and then store in the refrigerator for up to 1 month.

White kimchi

BAEK-KIMCHI

백 김 치

MAKES AROUND 3 KG (6 LB 12 OZ)

Preparation 1¼ hours
Resting 4 to 6 hours
+ 24 hours

INGREDIENTS

Brine

1 Chinese cabbage,
  approximately 2 kg
  (4 lb 8 oz)
200 g (7 oz) coarse sea
  salt
1 litre (4 cups) water

Marinade

½ pear
½ onion
50 g (1¾ oz) garlic cloves
60 g (2¼ oz) rice flour
  soup (page 90)
600 ml (2⅓ cups) mineral
  water
2 tablespoons fermented
  anchovy sauce
3 tablespoons ginger
  syrup (page 202)
1 tablespoon sea salt

Filling

200 g (7 oz) white radish
  (daikon), black radish
  or turnip
½ pear
½ carrot
½ red chilli (optional)
5 garlic chive stems
2 dried jujubes
1 tablespoon sea salt
1 tablespoon sugar

Gently cut and discard the hard end of the Chinese cabbage, ensuring the leaves remain attached together. Cut the cabbage into quarters. To do this, use a long, very sharp knife. Starting from the base, cut the cabbage two-thirds of the way to the top. Separate the two parts by hand, tearing the top of the leaves. Do the same for the two halves to obtain quarters of cabbage. Dilute 100 g (3½ oz) of the coarse sea salt in the 1 litre (4 cups) water, stirring vigorously to make the brine. Dip each cabbage quarter in brine, ensuring they are well moistened. Divide one handful of the remaining salt between the leaves around the firm base section of each cabbage quarter.

Place the cabbage quarters in a container with the remaining brine, with the inside of the leaves facing upwards. Leave for 3 to 5 hours, checking the elasticity of the leaves near the end. If the hard base of the leaves bends between two fingers without breaking, the brining is done. Rinse the cabbage three times in a row, then allow to drain for 1 hour minimum.

For the marinade, purée the pear, onion and garlic in a small food processor. Pour the blended mixture and the rice flour soup through a fine mesh sieve set over a bowl, pressing with a ladle while adding the mineral water to help extract the juice. When only the fibres remain in the sieve, discard them. If any water remains, add it to the strained juice. Season with the fermented anchovy sauce, ginger syrup and sea salt.

For the filling, cut the radish, pear, carrot and red chilli into matchsticks. Cut the chives into 5 cm (2 inch) pieces. Remove the central seed from the jujubes and cut into matchsticks. Mix all the ingredients with the sea salt and sugar.

Put 2 or 3 pinches of filling between each cabbage leaf and wrap each cabbage quarter up with the last outer leaf to keep the filling inside. Place the cabbages in an airtight container, with the inside of the leaves facing upwards, and cover with the marinade, making sure not to fill it more than 80% full. Close the lid tightly. Leave for 24 hours in the dark at room temperature and then store in the refrigerator for up to 6 months. You can eat this kimchi after 2 weeks.

NOTE —— *This kimchi is renowned for its digestive benefits.*

Kimchi stir-fry

KIMCHI-BOKKEUM

김치 볶음

This is a tasty recipe to make with well-fermented cabbage kimchi. I often quote it as an example when asked for advice on using kimchi as an ingredient, especially since it is a fairly simple dish to make.

SERVES 4

Preparation 5 minutes
Cooking 15 minutes

INGREDIENTS

*2 quarters Chinese
   cabbage kimchi (page 90)*
*3 cm (1¼ inches) leek
   (white part)*
*2 tablespoons neutral
   vegetable oil*
1½ tablespoons sugar
1 tablespoon sesame oil

Cut the cabbage kimchi quarters into 2 cm (¾ inch) wide strips. Chop the leek.

Coat a frying pan with the vegetable oil and stir-fry the leek over a high heat until fragrant. Add the kimchi and sugar to the pan. Stir-fry over a medium heat for 5 to 10 minutes, until the kimchi is half-softened. If the kimchi seems too dry, add 3 tablespoons water while cooking.

Turn off the heat but leave the pan on the hob or hotplate. Drizzle with the sesame oil, then mix together.

NOTE ——— *If this is being served as a side to another dish, simply sprinkle with thin slices of leek and sesame seeds. If serving it as a main course, add rice and 1 raw egg yolk, then sprinkle with chopped spring onion (scallion) and drizzle with 1 teaspoon sesame oil.*

KIMCHI
& PICKLES

Kimchi

If there is one dish that is associated with Korean food culture, it is kimchi. The word 'kimchi' refers to the lacto-fermentation process of vegetables in brine. There are several hundred varieties of kimchi, although the best known and most commonly consumed is 'baechu-kimchi' or Chinese cabbage kimchi (page 90). And for good reason, as it can be served as a side at most meals, but is also used as an ingredient in many Korean dishes.

A LITTLE BIT OF HISTORY

The history of kimchi dates back more than 2000 years, to a time when Koreans were already famous for their know-how in terms of fermentation. Vegetables seasoned and soaked in brine were placed in special pottery (ongi) containers that were buried to keep them away from light and heat. This allowed Koreans to eat vegetables during the harsh winters experienced on the peninsula. However, there was no chilli in the kimchi at the time. This was added later when chilli was imported into Korea by Portuguese merchants.

NATURAL LACTO-FERMENTATION

Kimchi is a living ingredient, comparable to cheese. When it is well preserved (in the refrigerator and not underground nowadays), it will develop its flavour and texture over several weeks to several months, depending on the vegetables used. The vegetables will be fresh and crunchy in the first few days, then will change over time through fermentation, without going bad. This result is achieved by the process of natural lacto-fermentation, aided by brine and the introduction of some key ingredients. The sometimes vinegary taste of kimchi is natural. There is never vinegar in kimchi, which is by no means a pickle (another way to preserve food for long periods). It is lacto-fermentation and the use of large amounts of garlic that give kimchi its healthy reputation. A reputation that extends far beyond Korean borders, especially when it is homemade.

KIMJANG – A FAMILY PRACTICE

Kimchi gave rise to a particular cultural practice in Korea called Kimjang. Kimjang is the word used to describe families when they gather in early autumn to prepare homemade kimchi together (sometimes several hundred cabbages are transformed into kimchi in one day). The fruit of the work is then shared among the family members, who will be able to enjoy it for months to come. This distinctively Korean ancestral practice, including the technique of preparing kimchi, is safeguarded by UNESCO as Intangible Cultural Heritage.

Pork and kimchi stir-fry

KIMCHI-JEYUK

김 치 제 육

This delicious dish made with cabbage kimchi and pork shoulder is very enjoyable shared with family or friends and accompanied by a bowl of makgeolli (Korean rice wine).

SERVES 4

Preparation 10 minutes
Resting 20 minutes
Cooking 40 minutes

INGREDIENTS

600 g (1 lb 5 oz) boneless
 pork shoulder
3 tablespoons sugar
350 g (12 oz) Chinese
 cabbage kimchi (page 90)
10 cm (4 inches) leek
 (white part)
50 ml (scant ¼ cup) white
 alcohol (soju or gin)
40 g (1½ oz) spicy
 marinade (page 148)
1 tablespoon fermented
 anchovy sauce

Tofu

200 g (7 oz) firm tofu
3 tablespoons neutral
 vegetable oil
Salt

Cut the pork into thin slices using a very sharp knife. It can be frozen for 4 hours before slicing. Marinate the pork slices in the sugar for 20 minutes. Cut the cabbage into 2 cm (¾ inch) wide strips. Cut the leek into 1 cm (½ inch) thick sections diagonally. Mix the kimchi, white alcohol and spicy marinade with the pork.

Heat a frying pan over a high heat and stir-fry the pork and kimchi mixture for 30 minutes. Add a little water during cooking if the mixture seems too dry. Add the leek and stir-fry for another 10 minutes. Season with the fermented anchovy sauce.

Meanwhile, cut the tofu into 1.5 cm (⅝ inch) rectangles. Heat a frying pan coated with the vegetable oil. Fry over a medium heat until all the sides are nicely golden. Use a spatula and a spoon to turn the tofu pieces so as not to break them. Season each side with salt while cooking. After cooking, let the tofu cool on paper towel.

Place a piece of kimchi and pork on a rectangle of tofu and eat together.

NOTE ——— *For a version that guests can enjoy making themselves, prepare salad leaves that they can fill with the stir-fry.*

Kimchi stew

KIMCHI-JJIGAE

김 치 찌 개

This kimchi-based dish is probably one of the most comforting for many Koreans. I enjoy it with a bowl of white rice topped with a fried egg.

SERVES 4
Preparation 10 minutes
Cooking 30 minutes

INGREDIENTS
500 g (1 lb 2 oz) Chinese
   cabbage kimchi (page 90)
300 g (10½ oz) boneless
   pork shoulder
1 onion
1 spring onion (scallion)
2 garlic cloves
200 g (7 oz) firm tofu
1 tablespoon sugar
2 tablespoons fermented
   anchovy sauce
500 ml (2 cups) water

Cut the kimchi into 2 cm (¾ inch) wide strips. Cut the pork shoulder into bite-sized pieces. Dice the onion. Cut the spring onion bulb into quarters and add to the onion. Cut the spring onion stem diagonally and set aside. Crush the garlic. Cut the firm tofu into 1 cm (½ inch) thick rectangles.

Heat a pot over a high heat without oil. When hot, add the kimchi and sprinkle with sugar. Put the pork on top and sprinkle evenly with the anchovy sauce. Add the crushed garlic. Sauté for a few minutes until the pork is golden and the kimchi begins to turn translucent. Add the water and diced onion, then mix.

Leave to simmer over a medium heat for 20 minutes, uncovered. Five minutes before the end of cooking, taste the broth and add more fermented anchovy sauce if needed. Add the tofu and spring onion stem. Serve hot.

Bossam kimchi and poached pork

BOSSAM

보 쌈

SERVES 4

Preparation 10 minutes
Resting 30 minutes
Cooking 50 minutes

INGREDIENTS

Poached pork

600 g (1 lb 5 oz) unseasoned pork belly

70 g (2½ oz) doenjang fermented
   soybean paste

4 garlic cloves

20 large black peppercorns

½ onion

4 green leaves from ½ leek

250 ml (1 cup) white alcohol (soju
   or gin)

Bossam kimchi

400 g (14 oz) white radish (daikon)

6 tablespoons sugar

1 tablespoon sea salt

½ pear

3 garlic chive stems (or 2 spring onion/
   scallion stems, no bulb)

3 garlic cloves

20 g (¾ oz) gochujang chilli paste

3 tablespoons gochugaru chilli powder

3 tablespoons fermented anchovy
   sauce

2 tablespoons ginger syrup (page 202)

Chinese cabbage side

¼ Chinese cabbage in brine, drained
   (see step 2 in Chinese cabbage kimchi
   recipe, page 90)

Bring 1.5 litres (6 cups) water to the boil in a pot. Cut the pork into two pieces lengthways and immerse in the boiling water. Add the doenjang, garlic, peppercorns, onion, leek leaves and alcohol. Simmer for 10 minutes over a high heat, covered, then 30 minutes over a medium heat, partially covered, then 10 minutes over a low heat.

While the pork is cooking, cut the white radish into 5 mm (¼ inch) matchsticks. Marinate with 5 tablespoons of the sugar and the sea salt for 30 minutes, mixing every 10 minutes. Rinse lightly under cold water, then drain and squeeze with your hands until no more liquid comes out.

Cut the pear into 5 mm (¼ inch) matchsticks and cut the chives into 3 cm (1¼ inch) pieces. Crush the garlic. In a bowl, mix the radish, pear, chives, garlic, gochujang, gochugaru, fermented anchovy sauce, 1 tablespoon of the sugar and the ginger syrup.

Drain the pork and slice thinly. Serve with the bossam kimchi. Arrange the cabbage in brine on the side after removing the first three outer leaves.

To eat, wrap the meat and bossam kimchi firmly in a cabbage leaf.

NOTE ——— *This dish is usually eaten at the end of the day after preparing cabbage kimchi, which explains why we keep a few quarters of the pickled cabbage aside. Instead of bossam kimchi, it is also possible to use the remaining Chinese cabbage kimchi marinade (page 90), ssamjang sauce (page 156) or a sauce made by mixing with 1 tablespoon fermented anchovy sauce, 1 crushed garlic clove, ⅓ chopped green chilli and 1 teaspoon gochugaru chilli powder.*

Puréed tofu kimchi stew

BIJI-JJIGAE

비 지 찌 개

This is definitely one of my favourite dishes for a weekday meal. I like to serve it together with several small dishes: grilled mackerel, kimchi, jangajji and seasoned gim seaweed sheets etc.

SERVES 4

Preparation 10 minutes
Cooking 30 minutes

INGREDIENTS

300 g (10½ oz) boneless
  pork shoulder
280 g (10 oz) Chinese
  cabbage kimchi (page 90)
2 garlic cloves
½ tablespoon sugar
½ tablespoon sesame oil
700 g (1 lb 9 oz) firm tofu
2 tablespoons neutral
  vegetable oil
1 teaspoon gochugaru
  chilli powder (optional)
400 ml (1½ cups) water
10 cm (4 inches) leek
  (white part)
2 tablespoons fermented
  anchovy sauce
Salt

Cut the pork shoulder into 1 cm (½ inch) cubes. Place the kimchi in a bowl and use scissors to cut it into small pieces. Crush the garlic and add to the kimchi along with the sugar and sesame oil. Add the pork and mix well with your hands. Crush the tofu with a potato masher, ensuring there are no large pieces remaining.

Heat the vegetable oil in a saucepan. When hot, add the pork and kimchi mixture. Sauté for 8 minutes, adding the gochugaru chilli powder for a spicier version.

Add the water. Bring to the boil and cook for 10 minutes. Meanwhile, cut the leek into thin strips. Add the crushed tofu to the saucepan with the fermented anchovy sauce. Cook for 5 minutes. Check the seasoning and adjust with salt as needed. Add the leek and cook for 5 minutes. Serve hot.

KIMCHI
& PICKLES

Cold kimchi noodles

BIBIM-GUKSU

비빔국수

*This is a meal that I used to enjoy eating with my mother when we happened
to be the only ones at home. It is a delightful dish that is eaten cold.*

FOR 2 BOWLS

Preparation 10 minutes
Cooking 20 minutes

INGREDIENTS

1 egg
120 g (4¼ oz) Chinese
cabbage kimchi (page 90)
1 teaspoon sugar
1 teaspoon sesame oil
5 cm (2 inches) cucumber
200 g (7 oz) somyeon
noodles (somen)

Sauce

60 g (2¼ oz) gochujang
chilli paste
5 tablespoons apple or
apple cider vinegar
3 tablespoons sugar
3 tablespoons soy sauce
2 teaspoons garlic powder
2 teaspoons sesame oil
2 teaspoons sesame seeds
1 pinch pepper

Immerse the egg in a saucepan of cold water and bring to the boil.
Cook for 9 minutes, then refresh the egg under cold water and
peel. Wash the kimchi and squeeze it in your hands to remove
the juice, then cut it into small pieces. Mix it well with the
sugar and sesame oil. Cut the cucumber into matchsticks.

Mix all the sauce ingredients together.

Bring salted water to the boil in a saucepan and tip in the somyeon
noodles. When the water is boiling again, add 200 ml (generous
¾ cup) cold water. Repeat this process a second time. At the third
boil, drain the noodles. Run them under cold water, using your hand
to swish them around to remove as much starch as possible.

Arrange the noodles in the middle of the serving bowls. Pour
some of the sauce into each bowl, then arrange the kimchi and
cucumber on top. Place a hard-boiled egg half in the middle
of each bowl. Mix all the ingredients together as you eat.

NOTE ——— *Eat with beef jangjorim (page 130) and sliced white radish
pickles (page 122). It also goes very well with Korean barbecue pork
(page 166).*

KIMCHI
& PICKLES

Chinese cabbage salad with kimchi sauce

BAECHU-GEOTJEORI

배추겉절이

SERVES 4

Preparation 15 minutes
Resting 2 hours

INGREDIENTS

600 g (1 lb 5 oz) Chinese
   cabbage
50 g (1¾ oz) coarse sea
   salt
1 litre (4 cups) water
4 garlic chive stems
   (or 2 spring onion/
   scallion stems, no bulb)
1 carrot
1 tablespoon sugar
50 g (1¾ oz) spicy
   marinade (page 148)
2 tablespoons fermented
   anchovy sauce
½ tablespoon sesame
   seeds
Sea salt

Cut the Chinese cabbage into large bite-sized pieces. Dissolve the salt in the water and immerse the cabbage. Leave to rest for 1½ hours.

Cut the chives into 5 cm (2 inch) pieces. Grate the carrot.

Drain the cabbage. Rinse it three times in a row, then allow to drain for 30 minutes. Mix it with the sugar, spicy marinade, fermented anchovy sauce, carrot and chives. Adjust the seasoning with sea salt. Sprinkle with sesame seeds.

NOTE ——— *Koreans eat this salad when there is no more kimchi in the fridge because it is much faster to prepare. However, it does not ferment and therefore does not keep for a long time. Ideally, it should be eaten within a week.*

Kimchi gimbap

KIMCHI-KIMBAP

김치김밥

I like gimbap recipes because there is an infinite number of variations you can make.
This kimchi-based version is the one I prepare most often at home.

FOR 2 ROLLS
Preparation 40 minutes
Cooking 10 minutes

INGREDIENTS
200 g (7 oz) Chinese
* cabbage kimchi*
* (page 90)*
3 teaspoons sugar
⅓ cucumber
2½ teaspoons salt, plus
* extra for seasoning*
3 eggs
1 teaspoon garlic powder
2 carrots
5 surimi (crab) sticks
½ tablespoon soy sauce
300 g (10½ oz) cooked
* white rice, warm (page 10)*
2 large gim seaweed
* sheets (nori)*
2 slices leg ham
Sesame oil
Neutral vegetable oil
Sesame seeds

Wash the kimchi and squeeze it in your hands to remove the juice, then cut it into small pieces. Mix it with 2 teaspoons of the sesame oil and 1 teaspoon of the sugar until well combined. Cut the cucumber into matchsticks, combine with ½ teaspoon of the salt, mix well and press using your hands to extract excess water.

Beat the eggs. Season with 1 pinch of salt and the garlic powder. Make 2 very thin omelettes in a hot oiled frying pan, then set aside. Cut the carrots into matchsticks. Stir-fry the carrots for 3 minutes in the hot oiled frying pan and season with 1 pinch of salt, then set aside. Shred the surimi sticks with your hands and stir-fry for 3 minutes in the hot oiled frying pan, adding 2 teaspoons of the sugar and the soy sauce while frying. Mix the rice with ½ tablespoon of the sesame oil and the remaining 2 teaspoons of salt (**A**).

To form the first roll, place 1 seaweed sheet on a bamboo mat (gimbal or makisu), rough side facing up. Cover the seaweed with a thin layer of evenly distributed rice. Arrange 1 slice of the ham on the rice, cutting it so it covers the surface of the sheet at the bottom. Place the omelette on top, cutting it in the same way. In the middle of the omelette, place some cucumber, surimi, carrot and kimchi side-by-side. Fold the lower part of the sheet using the mat (**B-C**) to cover the ingredients, pressing hard so that the rice sticks to the outside of the seaweed. On the top edge of the seaweed sheet, crush a few grains of rice to help properly close the gimbap (**D**). Repeat the process until the sheet has been fully rolled. Using a pastry brush, brush the top of the roll with sesame oil. Cut the roll into 1 cm (½ inch) thick sections (**E**). Repeat for the second roll. Sprinkle with sesame seeds and enjoy (**F**).

NOTE——— *Given that the rice and the ingredients are already well seasoned, gimbap is usually eaten without sauce.*

Soy sauce pickles

JANGAJJI

장아찌

FOR 3 JARS (500 ML/17 FL OZ) *Preparation 5 minutes – Cooking 5 minutes – Resting 24 hours*

MARINADE *200 ml (generous ¾ cup) soy sauce, 400 ml (1½ cups) beer, 200 ml (generous ¾ cup) white vinegar, 100 g (3½ oz) sugar*

Sterilise the jars. Pour water into a saucepan and place the jars in upside down. Heat over a high heat and boil for 5 minutes. Pick up the jars with oven mitts and wipe dry when they have cooled slightly. Fill each jar with the prepared vegetables. Place all the marinade ingredients in a saucepan. Bring to the boil and cook, uncovered, for 5 minutes over a high heat. Using a ladle, pour the hot marinade directly over the vegetables in the sterilised jars. Press down the vegetables a little with a spoon. Allow to cool to room temperature. Cover with plastic wrap, close the jars and store in the refrigerator. These pickles are ready to eat after 24 hours of resting and can be kept for at least 3 months.

Onion

INGREDIENTS
1 onion, 50 g (1¾ oz) white cabbage, ½ green chilli (optional)

Cut the onion and cabbage into 1.5 cm (⅝ inch) squares. Cut the chilli into 1.5 cm (⅝ inch) pieces. Place into a dry sterilised jar, then pour in the marinade.

Asparagus

INGREDIENTS
400 g (14 oz) asparagus

Remove the ends of the asparagus. Scrape the spears lightly with a knife to remove the ridges. Trim the asparagus to fit the jar, if necessary. Place the asparagus into a dry sterilised jar, then pour in the marinade.

Broccoli

INGREDIENTS
250 g (9 oz) broccoli, 1 teaspoon salt, 1 tablespoon white vinegar

Separate the broccoli into large bite-sized pieces, each including a head and stem portion. Soak for 20 minutes in cold water with the salt and vinegar. Drain and wash three times. Allow to drain. Place into a dry sterilised jar, then pour in the marinade.

KIMCHI
& PICKLES

Cucumber soy sauce pickles

OI JANGAJJI

오이 장아찌

FOR A 1 LITRE (35 FL OZ) JAR

Preparation 5 minutes
Cooking 5 minutes
Resting 1 week

INGREDIENTS

5 or 6 baby cucumbers
1 handful coarse sea salt
150 ml (generous ½ cup)
   soy sauce
150 ml (generous ½ cup)
   white vinegar
300 ml (1¼ cups) beer
75 g (2½ oz) sugar

Rub the cucumbers with the coarse sea salt. Rinse them under water and pat dry with paper towel.

Sterilise the jar. Pour water into a saucepan and place the jar in upside down. Heat over a high heat and boil for 5 minutes. Pick up the jar with oven mitts and wipe dry when it has cooled slightly.

Prepare the marinade. Pour the soy sauce, vinegar, beer and sugar into a saucepan. Bring to the boil and cook, uncovered, for 5 minutes over a high heat.

Place the cucumbers in the sterilised jar, packing them in as tightly as you can. Using a ladle, pour the hot marinade directly over the cucumbers. Push the cucumbers down a little with a spoon. Allow to cool to room temperature. Close the jar and store in the refrigerator.

These pickles are ready to eat after 1 week of resting and can be kept for at least 3 months.

NOTE ——— *The beer improves the preservation of the pickles while also making the vegetables crunchy. However, it is possible to replace it with the same amount of water.*

White radish pickles

MU-CHOJEOLIM

무 초 절 임

FOR 3 JARS (500 ML/ 17 FL OZ EACH)

Preparation 15 minutes
Cooking 5 minutes
Resting 24 hours

INGREDIENTS

1 kg (2 lb 4 oz) white
*   radish (daikon), black*
*   radish or turnip*
250 ml (1 cup) white
*   vinegar*
500 ml (2 cups) water
100 g (3½ oz) sugar
1 teaspoon sea salt

Peel the radish and chop into three equal sections. Cut the first third into very thin slices using a mandolin. Do the same with the second third, then cut each slice into three strips. Cut the last third into about 1.5 cm (⅝ inch) cubes.

Sterilise the jars. Pour water into a saucepan and place the jars in upside down. Heat over a high heat and boil for 5 minutes. Pick up the jars with oven mitts and wipe dry when they have cooled slightly.

Fill each jar with one of the different radish shapes.

Make the marinade. Pour the vinegar, water, sugar and salt into a saucepan. Bring to the boil. When the sugar and salt are well dissolved, pour the hot marinade into each jar up to the level of the radish. Push the radish down a little with a spoon. Allow to cool to room temperature, cover with plastic wrap, then close the jars and store in the refrigerator.

These pickles are ready to eat after 24 hours of resting and can be kept for at least 3 months.

TIPS —— *The round-shaped pickles are often served with ssambap (page 156). They can also be wrapped in a large lettuce leaf or used in a hamburger. The strips can be served as a side to temper spicy dishes. They can also be mixed with cold kimchi noodles (page 112) instead of Chinese cabbage kimchi. The cubes are also good as a side to temper spicy cuisine. They are eaten with Korean fried chicken (page 56).*

KIMCHI & PICKLES

MEAT & POULTRY
육류와 가금류

*Marinated, grilled, crumbed, simmered or raw . . .
Korean cuisine has many ways to serve meat. In this
chapter, you will also find everything you need to know
to prepare an authentic Korean barbecue at home.*

Braised Korean chicken

DAKBOKKEUMTANG
닭 볶 음 탕

When I have tteokbokki tteok at home, I love adding some to this dish just before the end of the cooking time. It adds a pleasant texture and rounds out the dish so there is no need to serve it with rice.

SERVES 4
Preparation 20 minutes
Resting 20 minutes
Cooking 50 minutes

INGREDIENTS
1.2 kg (2 lb 10 oz) whole
　chicken
2 tablespoons sugar
2 tablespoons ginger syrup
　(page 202)
4 medium potatoes
2 carrots
1 onion
10 cm (4 inches) leek
　(white part)
100 g (3½ oz) spicy
　marinade (page 148)
100 ml (scant ½ cup) soy
　sauce
400 ml (1½ cups) water
100 ml (scant ½ cup) white
　alcohol (soju or gin)

Clean the chicken well to remove any remaining feathers or down. Remove any excess fat and skin with scissors and discard the parson's nose. Cut through the neck to cut the chicken in half lengthways. Cut off the wings, thighs and drumsticks. Cut each chicken half in two or three widthways, leaving the chicken breast attached to the carcass pieces.

Combine the cut chicken with the sugar and ginger syrup. Leave to rest for 20 minutes. Meanwhile, peel and cut the potatoes in half, the carrots in 2 cm (¾ inch) sections and the onion in quarters. Cut the leek into 2 cm (¾ inch) pieces.

After 20 minutes of resting, add the spicy marinade and soy sauce to the chicken. Mix to coat the chicken with the sauce. Place the chicken in a saucepan, add the potato, carrot, onion, water and alcohol. Bring to the boil and cook, covered, for 10 minutes over a high heat, then stir. Switch to a medium heat and open the lid slightly. Leave to simmer for 30 minutes, stirring regularly. Add the leek and simmer for another 10 minutes.

MEAT &
POULTRY

Korean alcohols

In Korea, we always prepare dishes to share when we drink alcohol. This combination of food and alcohol is a hallmark of our culture. I was born in Seoul, a city that never sleeps. There, you can eat and drink all night long, and reasonably cheaply too. I really enjoyed this festive lifestyle with my friends and family and sometimes miss this part of Korean culture, which is why I like to re-create it at home.

EVERYDAY ALCOHOLS

First of all, here are the three most consumed alcohols in Korea. **Soju** is definitely the most well-known Korean alcohol around the world. Each region has its own variations and it is quite strong (between 16.5% and 21% alcohol). The most famous brand is called Chamisul. You can drink it with ice cubes but it is traditionally served in a small glass to drink it straight or mixed with beer, a mixture called 'somek' (the ideal proportion is 3 parts soju to 7 parts beer). Nowadays there are also many flavoured varieties with a lower alcohol content. Enjoy with Korean barbecue pork (page 166), marinated or sautéed meats and stews. **Makgeolli** is a syrupy rice alcohol that is slightly sparkling as a result of fermentation. It is drunk in wide, flat bowls and is enjoyed with Korean pancakes or kimchi dishes. **Mekju** are blonde and light Korean beers that go with most dishes, but I like to drink them with fritters and Korean fried chicken (page 56).

RICE-BASED YAK-JU

Yak-ju is a distilled rice alcohol that is often touted for its medicinal virtues. It usually contains herbs and fruits that have traditional pharmaceutical uses. There is a polite greeting for the elderly in Korea that translates as: 'Did you drink a yak-ju yesterday?' so as not to imply that the person might be overly fond of a drink! **Cheong-ju** is a traditional rice alcohol, which is often drunk during the major holidays of Chuseok and Seollal (the Korean equivalents of celebrations like Christmas and New Year) and is served with pancakes, soups and stews. **Baekse-ju** is a rice alcohol with goji berries, ginseng and 10 other roots and medicinal plants. It can be enjoyed with Korean chicken soup (page 144), steamed sea bream (page 176), bossam kimchi and poached pork (page 108) and other healthy dishes. **Sansachun** is a rice alcohol made with hawthorn berries and renowned for its digestive virtues. I like to serve it with meat dishes. The name **Bokbunja-ju** comes from the Korean word for 'black raspberry'. It is a fairly sweet alcohol that goes well with desserts and sweet-and-sour dishes. It is known for giving energy and can be enjoyed with Korean beef tartare (page 132), Korean beef patties (page 152) and desserts such as yakgwa biscuits (page 196) or sweet rice balls (page 192). **Maechuisun** and **maehwasu** are mild sweet spirits that contain green plum and are best enjoyed with light vegetable dishes.

Beef jangjorim

SOGOGI JANGJORIM

소 고 기 장 조 림

I like to prepare this shredded beef recipe in advance. I then always have a portion on hand in the refrigerator so that I have something delicious to eat when I'm very busy.

FOR A 750 ML (26 FL OZ) JAR

Preparation 25 minutes
Resting 1½ hours
Cooking 1½ hours

INGREDIENTS

1 kg (2 lb 4 oz) hanger steak (onglet)
2 litres (8 cups) water
100 ml (scant ½ cup) white alcohol (soju or gin)
3 green leek leaves
1 onion
20 large black peppercorns
50 g (1¾ oz) garlic cloves
10 g (¼ oz) fresh ginger
200 ml (generous ¾ cup) soy sauce
50 g (1¾ oz) sugar

Cut the meat into approximately 15 cm (6 inch) wide sections. Soak in cold water for 1½ hours to draw out the blood, changing the water every 30 minutes. Bring water to the boil in a pot. Immerse the meat pieces in the water and boil for 5 minutes, then drain and wash under running water, taking care to remove the clotted blood.

Pour the 2 litres (8 cups) of water and the alcohol into a pot. Secure the leek leaves, whole onion, peppercorns, garlic and peeled ginger in a cotton muslin bag. Place the bag in the pot and bring to the boil. Add the meat. Simmer for 50 minutes over a medium heat, partially covered.

Remove the muslin bag and discard its contents. Set the meat and broth aside separately. Allow the broth to cool until the fat solidifies on the surface, then pass through a fine mesh sieve to remove the fat. Shred the meat with your hands in the direction of the muscle fibres to obtain strips about 5 mm (¼ inch) thick.

Bring 800 ml (3¼ cups) of the broth, the soy sauce, sugar and meat to the boil in a pot. Cook for 25 minutes over a medium heat. Pour the meat and juice into a pre-sterilised jar (page 118). Allow to cool to room temperature. This beef keeps for 2 weeks in the refrigerator. Serve as a side or as a filling, cold or slightly warmed.

TIP —— *A nice way to eat this beef jangjorim is to put rice in a bowl, then add the beef on top with 15 g (½ oz) butter and 1 fried egg, and pour the sauce over the top. Mix and enjoy.*

MEAT & POULTRY

Korean beef tartare

YUKHOE

육회

A sip of yak-ju. A bite of yukhoe. A sip of yak-ju . . . Discover this wonderful explosion of flavours!

SERVES 2
Preparation 25 minutes

INGREDIENTS
2 garlic cloves
1.5 cm (⅝ inch) leek
  (white part)
½ Korean pear
  (or ½ green pear)
300 g (10½ oz) extra-
  fresh beef fillet or sirloin
2 tablespoons mat
  ganjang sauce
  (page 146)
1 tablespoon sesame oil
1 tablespoon sugar
½ tablespoon sesame
  seeds (or pine nuts), plus
  extra for sprinkling
50 g (1¾ oz) rocket
  (arugula)
1 egg yolk
Salt and pepper

Crush the garlic. Chop the leek. Peel the pear and cut into 5 mm (¼ inch) thick matchsticks. Pat the meat with paper towel to remove any excess blood. Cut the beef into sticks of the same thickness.

Mix the meat with the garlic, leek, mat ganjang, sesame oil, sugar, sesame seeds or pine nuts, salt and pepper using chopsticks or forks. Avoid mixing by hand so as to not alter the colour of the meat due to body heat.

Arrange the rocket leaves on a plate. Place the pear matchsticks on top. Press the meat into a bowl and then tip it onto the pear. Press lightly in the middle of the meat to create an indent and gently slide the egg yolk in. Sprinkle with the extra sesame seeds or pine nuts.

Eat by piercing the egg yolk and using it as a sauce to dip pieces of meat into.

TIP —— *If any of this dish is left at the end of the meal, keep it in the refrigerator. You can pan-fry it the next day with a little mat ganjang. Enjoy with rice.*

MEAT & POULTRY

Pork bulgogi

DWAEJI-BULGOGI

돼 지 불 고 기

This is a delicious recipe combining pork and chilli, but it also becomes a three-in-one dish when you make a bigger quantity. Combine it with a bowl of rice and vegetables, a bibimbap or ramyeon – instant Korean noodles.

SERVES 4

Preparation 25 minutes
Resting 20 minutes
Cooking 30 minutes

INGREDIENTS

700 g (1 lb 9 oz) pork shoulder
2 tablespoons ginger syrup (page 202)
1 tablespoon sugar
1 carrot
⅓ zucchini (courgette)
1 onion
10 cm (4 inches) leek (white part)
60 g (2¼ oz) spicy marinade (page 148)
20 g (¾ oz) gochujang chilli paste
6 tablespoons soy sauce
1 tablespoon fermented anchovy sauce
2 tablespoons white alcohol (soju or gin)

Thinly slice the pork. Marinate the pork slices in the ginger syrup and sugar for 20 minutes.

Cut the carrot into three sections, then each section in half lengthways and lastly into strips lengthways. Cut the zucchini into two sections, then each section in half lengthways and lastly into strips lengthways. Cut the onion in half, then into 1 cm (½ inch) wide slices. Cut the leek into 1 cm (½ inch) sections diagonally.

Mix the meat with the spicy marinade, gochujang, soy sauce, fermented anchovy sauce and alcohol. Heat a frying pan. When hot, add the meat and stir-fry for 20 minutes over a high heat. Add the vegetables. Stir-fry for 10 minutes. When the vegetables have softened slightly, serve hot. You can also eat this like ssambap (page 156), if desired.

TIP —— *In order to easily slice the meat, allow it to firm up for 3 to 4 hours in the freezer before cutting.*

Beef japchae

JAPCHAE

잡 채

This generous beef and vermicelli recipe is an iconic dish in Korea, and is often cooked for family celebrations.

SERVES 4

Preparation 25 minutes
Resting 2 hours
Cooking 40 minutes

INGREDIENTS

200 g (7 oz) sweet potato
* vermicelli*
300 g (10½ oz) thick beef
* steak*
6 tablespoons soy sauce
4 tablespoons sugar
1½ teaspoons garlic
* powder*
1 teaspoon pepper
1 red capsicum (pepper)
1 carrot
½ zucchini (courgette)
4 pyogo mushrooms
* (shiitake) or oyster*
* mushrooms*
½ onion
3 cm (1¼ inches) leek
* (white part)*
1 egg
100 ml (scant ½ cup)
* water*
4 tablespoons sesame oil
½ tablespoon sesame
* seeds*
5 garlic chives
Neutral vegetable oil
Salt

Immerse the sweet potato vermicelli in cold water and leave to soak for 2 hours, then drain.

Cut the meat into thin strips. Marinate with 2 tablespoons of the soy sauce, 1 tablespoon of the sugar, ½ teaspoon of the garlic powder and ½ teaspoon of the pepper while you prepare the rest of the dish.

Cut the capsicum, carrot and zucchini into matchsticks. Thinly slice the mushrooms and onion. Chop the leek. Beat the egg with a good pinch of salt. Cook a thin omelette in a hot oiled frying pan. Allow to cool, roll it up gently and cut into thin strips.

Heat more vegetable oil in the frying pan over a high heat. Stir-fry the carrot and zucchini, seasoning them with a pinch of salt. When the vegetables have softened slightly, set them aside in a bowl. Do the same with the capsicum, then the mushrooms, then the onion. Stir-fry the marinated meat for 5 minutes. Set everything aside in the same bowl.

Prepare the sauce. Combine the water, 4 tablespoons of the soy sauce, 3 tablespoons of the sugar, 1 teaspoon of the garlic powder and ½ teaspoon of the pepper. Heat 2 tablespoons of the sesame oil and the chopped leek in a large pan over a medium heat. When the leek becomes aromatic, add the vermicelli and sauce. Cook, stirring, for 5 minutes.

Pour the hot vermicelli into the bowl of vegetables. Cut the vermicelli with scissors, in one direction then in the other. Add the sesame seeds and 2 tablespoons of the sesame oil and mix gently with your hands when the vermicelli have cooled slightly. Arrange the japchae on plates. Top the japchae off with the omelette strips and garnish with chopped garlic chives.

MEAT &
POULTRY

Grilled pork maekjeok

MAEKJEOK

맥 적

I have created my own twist on this very old marinated pork recipe by adding a hint of lemon. You can also make it on the barbecue.

SERVES 4
Preparation 15 minutes
Cooking 30 minutes

INGREDIENTS
3 green leek leaves
700 g (1 lb 9 oz) pork shoulder (bone in)
80 g (2¾ oz) doenjang fermented soybean paste
2 tablespoons mat ganjang sauce (page 146)
3 tablespoons preserved lemon (page 198)
1 teaspoon ground ginger
2 tablespoons white alcohol (soju or gin)
1 tablespoon sesame oil

Cut the leek leaves into 7 cm (2¾ inch) pieces. Cut the pork shoulder into 2 cm (¾ inch) thick slices. Using a knife, score each slice on both sides, making a grid pattern. Be careful not to cut through the slices. Mix the meat slices and leek pieces with the doenjang, mat ganjang, preserved lemon, ginger, alcohol and sesame oil.

Preheat the oven to 180°C (350°F). Place the pork slices, without overlapping, on a grill rack with a roasting pan underneath. Place the pieces of leek around the meat with a few slices of preserved lemon, if desired. Cook for 30 minutes.

After removing from the oven, discard the leek pieces. Cut the meat into small bite-sized pieces using scissors. You can eat it like ssambap (page 156) if you like.

NOTE ——— *Serve this dish with rice, soy sauce pickles (page 118), any type of kimchi and ssamjang sauce (page 156).*

MEAT & POULTRY

Spicy beef and vegetable soup

YUKGAEJANG

육 개 장

I like to prepare this spicy beef soup every winter. Without it, this season often seems endless to me!

SERVES 4
Preparation 25 minutes
Resting 2 hours
Cooking 1 hour

INGREDIENTS
500 g (1 lb 2 oz) hanger
*   steak (onglet)*
1.5 litres (6 cups) water
50 ml (scant ¼ cup)
*   white alcohol*
*   (soju or gin)*
3 garlic cloves
2 green leek leaves
100 g (3½ oz) spicy
*   marinade (page 148)*
3 tablespoons mat
*   ganjang sauce*
*   (page 146)*
200 g (7 oz) bean sprouts
5 pyogo mushrooms
*   (shiitake) or oyster*
*   mushrooms*
25 cm (10 inches) leek
*   (white part)*
1 tablespoon sesame oil
1 tablespoon neutral
*   vegetable oil*
3 tablespoons soy sauce
½ teaspoon pepper
Salt

Cut the meat into approximately 15 cm (6 inch) wide pieces. Soak the meat in cold water for 1½ hours to draw out the blood, changing the water every 30 minutes, then drain. Bring the 1.5 litres (6 cups) water to the boil. Add the meat, alcohol, peeled garlic cloves and green leek leaves. Cook over a medium heat for 40 minutes without covering after boiling has resumed.

Using a spoon, remove the foam from the surface of the broth. Separate the broth from the meat, discarding the garlic and green leek leaves but reserving the broth. When the meat is cool enough, shred it using your hands. Mix it with the spicy marinade and mat ganjang. Allow to stand.

Meanwhile, wash the bean sprouts. Cut the mushrooms into 1.5 cm (⅝ inch) slices. Cut the leek white into five sections of 5 cm (2 inches) each, then each section in half lengthways and each half section in four lengthways (a width of 1 cm/½ inch is ideal).

Heat the sesame oil and vegetable oil in a saucepan. When it heats up, add the meat and stir-fry for 3 minutes. Add the leek white and soy sauce and mix well, then add about 1 litre (4 cups) of the reserved broth. Cook over a high heat for 10 minutes after boiling has resumed. Add the mushrooms and bean sprouts and boil for a further 10 minutes. Season with salt and the pepper.

NOTE —— *You can serve this dish with rice and vegetable or fish side dishes.*

MEAT &
POULTRY

Beef and Chinese cabbage doenjang soup

SOGOGI BAECHU DOENJANG-GUK

소 고 기 배 추 된 장 국

This is a tasty soup made of cabbage, beef and fermented soybean paste that I usually enjoy in the morning before a day's work.

SERVES 4
Preparation 15 minutes
Cooking 30 minutes

INGREDIENTS
½ Chinese cabbage
300 g (10½ oz) thick beef steak
4 garlic cloves
1 tablespoon sesame oil
2 tablespoons mat ganjang sauce (page 146)
1 litre (4 cups) water
70 g (2½ oz) doenjang fermented soybean paste

Cut the half Chinese cabbage into two quarters. Remove the base. Cut each quarter into approximately 2 cm (¾ inch) wide pieces. Wash and drain. Pat the beef with paper towel to absorb excess blood. Cut the beef into bite-sized pieces. Crush the garlic.

Heat the sesame oil in a pot over a high heat. Add the meat, garlic and mat ganjang. Sauté until the outside of the beef is cooked. Pour in the water and bring to the boil. Add the cabbage and doenjang. Leave to simmer for another 15 minutes over a medium heat.

NOTE —— *Serve this soup with rice, stir-fried green beans (page 64) or a variety of kimchi.*

MEAT & POULTRY

Korean chicken soup

YEONGGYE-BAEKSUK

영 계 백 숙

SERVES 3

Preparation 25 minutes
Cooking 1 hour

INGREDIENTS

3 poussins
2 heads garlic
¼ turnip
20 large black peppercorns
3 green leek leaves
½ onion
10 g (¼ oz) fresh ginger
2 litres (8 cups) water
100 ml (scant ½ cup) white
* alcohol (soju or gin)*
20 g (¾ oz) goji berries
3 dried jujubes
60 chive stems
5 cm (2 inches) leek
* (white part)*
Sesame seeds
Salt and pepper

Clean the poussins well to remove any remaining feathers or down. Remove any excess fat and skin with scissors. Detach and discard the parson's nose.

Peel the garlic cloves. Place the turnip, peppercorns, leek leaves, onion, ginger and half the garlic in a cotton muslin bag and secure. Pour the water into a saucepan and place the bag in the water. Bring to the boil. Immerse the poussins in the boiling water and add the alcohol. Return to the boil, reduce the heat to medium and cook for 20 minutes. Add the remaining garlic, goji berries and jujubes. Cook for 20 minutes.

Reduce the heat to low and cook for another 10 minutes. Using a spoon, remove the fat from the surface of the broth. Serve each poussin in an individual bowl. Add the broth with the garlic, jujube and goji berries. Add 20 chive stalks and thin slices of leek white to each bowl.

Enjoy with a mixture of salt, pepper and a pinch of sesame seeds served in a small dish for each guest. Tear off pieces of the poussin and dip into this mixture. You can also season the soup with this mixture, if desired.

TIPS —— *To finish the broth, it is customary to add rice once there is no meat left. Serve this soup with white radish kimchi (page 94) or chive kimchi (page 96).*

NOTE —— *Samgyetang is another soup using a whole poussin, which differs from this one by the addition of ginseng. If you want to make a samgyetang, you can add fresh or powdered ginseng root (10 g/¼ oz) to the pan at the same time as the poussin.*

Mat ganjang sauce

MAT GANJANG

맛 간 장

This reworked soy sauce recipe is truly magic. It enhances all dishes that use traditional soy sauce.

FOR A 250 ML (9 FL OZ) JAR

Preparation 15 minutes
Cooking 20 minutes
Resting 15 minutes

INGREDIENTS

¼ onion

¼ turnip

2 green leek leaves

⅓ lemon

⅓ apple

4 garlic cloves

170 ml (⅔ cup) soy sauce

130 ml (½ cup) water

65 ml (¼ cup) white
  alcohol (soju or gin)

1 tablespoon fermented
  anchovy sauce

10 large black
  peppercorns

Peel the onion and turnip. Roughly chop the leek leaves. Cut thin rounds of lemon and thin slices of apple. Peel the garlic cloves.

Bring the soy sauce, water, alcohol, fermented anchovy sauce, turnip, leek, onion, garlic and peppercorns to the boil in a saucepan, covered. Simmer for 10 minutes over a medium heat. Add the lemon and apple and simmer for 10 minutes, covered.

Turn off the heat and remove the lid. Allow to cool for 15 minutes. Strain the sauce with a fine mesh sieve. Crush the ingredients to get as much juice out as possible, then discard. Pour the sauce into a pre-sterilised jar or bottle (page 118).

Allow to cool to room temperature before closing the jar or bottle. Keeps for about 3 weeks in the refrigerator.

MEAT &
POULTRY

Spicy marinade

MAEUN YANGNYEOMJANG

매운 양념장

FOR A 750 ML (26 FL OZ) JAR

Preparation 10 minutes

INGREDIENTS

2 onions

2 heads garlic

260 g (9¼ oz) gochugaru chilli powder

200 ml (generous ¾ cup) fermented anchovy sauce

200 ml (generous ¾ cup) ginger syrup (page 202)

Peel the onions and process in a small food processor. Peel the garlic cloves and crush.

Mix the garlic and onion with the gochugaru, fermented anchovy sauce and ginger syrup. The consistency should be quite thick. If the marinade is too liquid, add more gochugaru. Pour the sauce into a pre-sterilised jar or bottle (page 118).

This sauce keeps for about 6 months in the refrigerator.

TIP —— *If you need to wet the onion to process it properly, use anchovy sauce instead of water.*

Barbecue marinade

BULGOGI YANGNYEOM

불 고 기 양 념

FOR 700 G (1 LB 9 OZ) MEAT

Preparation 10 minutes

INGREDIENTS

1 onion

5 g (⅛ oz) fresh ginger

½ pear

6 garlic cloves

100 ml (scant ½ cup) soy sauce

50 ml (scant ¼ cup) white alcohol (soju or gin)

2 tablespoons honey

35 g (1¼ oz) sugar

1 teaspoon pepper

Peel the onion and ginger. Peel and remove the core from the pear. Peel the garlic cloves. Process everything together in a small food processor.

Combine the processed ingredients with the soy sauce, alcohol, honey, sugar and pepper.

This sauce can be kept for 1 week in the refrigerator. However, it is best to marinate the meat just after the sauce has been made. The marinated meat can be kept for 2 days.

MEAT & POULTRY

Beef bulgogi ssambap

BULGOGI SSAMBAP

불고기 쌈밥

The recipe for bulgogi embodies the soul of Korean cuisine. Eaten like ssambap (page 156), this is a wonderful dish to share with friends and family.

SERVES 4

Preparation 25 minutes
Resting 12 hours
Cooking 10 minutes

INGREDIENTS

700 g (1 lb 9 oz) prime rib
  of beef, very thinly sliced
Barbecue marinade
  (page 148)
1 tablespoon sesame oil
½ onion
3 pyogo mushrooms
  (shiitake) or button
  mushrooms
½ carrot
10 cm (4 inches) leek
  (white part)

Ssambap filling

½ cos lettuce
Cooked white rice, hot
  (page 10)
Ssamjang sauce
  (page 156)
1 endive
White radish pickles
  (page 122)

Cut the thinly sliced beef into bite-sized strips. Pour the barbecue marinade and sesame oil over the meat and mix to coat the meat well. Leave to rest in the refrigerator for at least 12 hours.

Cut the onion and mushrooms into strips, the carrot into matchsticks and the leek white into 5 mm (¼ inch) slices diagonally.

Heat a frying pan. When it is hot, place the meat and marinade into the pan and spread over the entire surface. Add the vegetables. Stir regularly for about 10 minutes until the meat is completely cooked.

Wash the cos leaves and fill with a bite-sized amount of rice and a touch of ssamjang sauce. Wash the endive leaves and fill with a slice of the white radish pickles, a bite-sized amount of rice and a touch of ssamjang sauce. Eat the leaves filled with the meat.

The meat can be kept raw in its marinade in the refrigerator for up to 2 days.

TIP——— *If you run out of time, you can simply serve this dish with a bowl of white rice.*

MEAT &
POULTRY

Korean beef patties

TTEOKGALBI

떡 갈 비

MAKES 6 PATTIES

Preparation 10 minutes
Cooking 15 minutes

INGREDIENTS

1 onion
½ carrot
600 g (1 lb 5 oz) beef
  mince
6 tablespoons soy sauce
4 tablespoons sugar
2 tablespoons ginger
  syrup (page 202)
1 tablespoon sesame oil
1 teaspoon salt
1 pinch pepper
1 egg yolk
1 tablespoon water
Chives
Pine nuts

Finely chop the onion and carrot. Pat the meat with paper towel to remove any excess blood. Mix the meat with the onion, carrot, soy sauce, sugar, ginger syrup, sesame oil, salt, pepper and egg yolk until well combined. The texture should be like a paste.

Divide into six portions. Flatten each portion in your hands to obtain even-shaped patties about 1 cm (½ inch) thick. Press in the middle of each patty with your thumb to create an indent.

Heat a frying pan. When it is hot, place the patties in the pan with the indent facing up. Cook for a total of 5 minutes, turning regularly to prevent the meat from burning. Add the water. Cover and cook for 10 minutes, turning halfway through.

Serve on a bed of chives and sprinkle with some crushed pine nuts.

NOTE ——— *I also like to use this beef mince recipe to make burgers by adding a few white radish pickle slices (page 122) instead of gherkins, seasonal vegetables, Cheddar cheese and mayonnaise.*

Thinly sliced grilled ribs

LA GALBI

LA 갈비

LA galbi is always the first dish I eat when I return to Korea. My mother prepares it for me as soon as I arrive to welcome me. It's a family tradition that we have shared since I left.

SERVES 4

Preparation 10 minutes
Resting 14 hours
Cooking 15 minutes

INGREDIENTS

1 kg (2 lb 4 oz) beef short
* ribs with bones, cut into*
* thin slices*
20 cm (8 inches) leek
* (white part)*
1 kiwifruit
Barbecue marinade
* (page 148)*
3 tablespoons soy sauce
1 tablespoon sesame oil

Immerse the meat in a bowl of cold water and leave for 2 hours, changing the water every 30 minutes before draining.

Cut the leek into four pieces, then cut each piece in half lengthways. Peel and purée the kiwifruit in a small food processor. Pour the barbecue marinade, the soy sauce, kiwi and sesame oil over the meat and mix to coat well. Mix with the leek. Leave to rest in the refrigerator for at least 12 hours.

Heat a cast-iron chargrill pan or frying pan over a high heat. Place the meat slices and leek pieces into the pan. Cook for 7 minutes on each side over a medium heat.

Cut the meat between the pieces of bone with scissors before serving. You can eat this like ssambap (page 156), if desired, or simply with rice and Chinese cabbage kimchi (page 90).

NOTE —— *The meat can be kept raw in its marinade in the refrigerator for up to 3 days.*

MEAT &
POULTRY

Korean ssambap table

SSAMBAP

쌈 밥

Ssambap is not just a dish, it is a way of eating in Korea, a meal that is eaten in the manner of the 'ssam'. The principle is to pack cooked rice ('bap' in Korean) and other ingredients to each person's liking into a lettuce and/or cabbage leaf at the table.

The recipe I am including here is for ssamjang sauce, which is essential when preparing ssambap at home. You will also need to set the table with:

• a meat recipe: Korean barbecue pork (page 166), pork bulgogi (page 134), grilled pork maekjeok (page 138) or beef bulgogi (page 150)
• small side dishes: kimchi, pickles, raw and cooked vegetables
• a stew recipe: most often doenjang vegetable stew (page 158)
• several varieties of green salad
• ½ steamed white cabbage
• a bowl of rice

To eat, take a large lettuce leaf and arrange a steamed white cabbage leaf on top (**A-B**), then add some rice, a touch of ssamjang sauce, a piece of meat and 1 or 2 small side dishes of your choice (**C**). Wrap the outer leaf around the filling (**D-E**), then enjoy (**F**).

Steamed white cabbage

SERVES 4
Preparation 5 minutes
Cooking 25 minutes

INGREDIENTS
½ white cabbage

Discard the outer leaves of the cabbage. Cut into two quarters, wash and drain. Place a steamer tray or basket in a saucepan. Add water to come up to 1 cm (½ inch) below the tray. Place the cabbage quarters on one of the inner sides. Cover and bring to the boil over a high heat, then lower the heat to medium and cook for 15 to 20 minutes. Turn off the heat and stand for 5 minutes, covered.

Ssamjang sauce

SERVES 4
Preparation 10 minutes

INGREDIENTS
40 g (1½ oz) gochujang chilli paste,
30 g (1 oz) doenjang fermented soybean paste,
1 teaspoon sugar, 1 tablespoon sesame oil,
½ tablespoon sesame seeds, 2 crushed garlic cloves

Mix all the ingredients together. The sauce will keep for 2 weeks in a sealed container in the fridge.

MEAT & POULTRY

A

B

C

D

E

F

Doenjang vegetable stew

DOENJANG-JJIGAE

된 장 찌 개

This stew made with vegetables and fermented soybean paste is ideal as a side to a Korean barbecue.

SERVES 4
Preparation 15 minutes
Cooking 20 minutes

INGREDIENTS
600 ml (2⅓ cups) water
*12 cm (4½ inch) square
    dasima seaweed (kombu)*
1 carrot
1 onion
½ zucchini (courgette)
½ leek (white part)
*150 g (5½ oz) mangadak
    mushrooms (shimeji) or
    button mushrooms*
½ green chilli
*100 g (3½ oz) doenjang
    fermented soybean
    paste*
250 g (9 oz) firm tofu
*1 teaspoon gochugaru
    chilli powder (optional)*

Heat the water in a saucepan over a high heat. Clean the piece of dasima seaweed under running water and add it to the saucepan.

Cut the carrot into 1 cm (½ inch) thick quarter rounds. Roughly chop the onion. When the water boils, add the carrot and onion.

Cut the zucchini into 1.5 cm (⅝ inch) thick quarter rounds and add them to the broth as soon as boiling resumes. Cook for 10 minutes. Meanwhile, cut the leek into 1 cm (½ inch) thick diagonal slices and the tofu into 2 cm (¾ inch) thick cubes. Remove the mangadak mushroom stems and wash them (for button mushrooms, cut into quarters). Cut the chilli into 1 cm (½ inch) thick sections and wash well under running water while removing the seeds.

After 10 minutes, add the doenjang, leek, mushrooms, tofu and chilli. When boiling resumes, simmer for 5 minutes. Finish the seasoning by adding more doenjang to your taste. For a spicier version, add the gochugaru chilli powder.

MEAT &
POULTRY

Lettuce salad with kimchi sauce

SANGCHU-GEOTJEORI

상추겉절이

This is a side dish I often prepare instead of kimchi or small vegetable dishes when we have an impromptu barbecue.

SERVES 4
Preparation 10 minutes

INGREDIENTS
½ lettuce
½ onion
½ carrot
1 tablespoon gochugaru
   chilli powder
2 tablespoons soy sauce
1 tablespoon fermented
   anchovy sauce
3 tablespoons apple or
   apple cider vinegar
2 tablespoons sugar
1 teaspoon garlic powder
1 tablespoon sesame oil
½ tablespoon sesame
   seeds

Wash the lettuce, drain it and roughly tear the leaves. Thinly slice the onion and immerse in a bowl of water with a few drops of vinegar. Allow to soak for 5 minutes before draining. Cut the carrot into matchsticks.

Mix the lettuce with the onion, carrot, gochugaru, soy sauce, fermented anchovy sauce, apple vinegar, sugar, garlic powder, sesame oil and sesame seeds. Serve.

NOTE ——— *This salad is best eaten as soon as it is made. You can serve it with grilled or sautéed marinated meat or as a side instead of kimchi.*

MEAT &
POULTRY

Leek salad

PA-MUCHIM
파 무 침

The combination of leek and grilled pork belly is a real delight. Although cutting the leek may seem a bit long when you are preparing it, once the dish is served you will realise the effort really was worth it.

SERVES 4

Preparation 20 minutes
Resting 10 minutes

INGREDIENTS

4 leeks (white part)
1 tablespoon gochugaru chilli powder
2 tablespoons soy sauce
1 tablespoon fermented anchovy sauce
4 tablespoons apple or apple cider vinegar
2 tablespoons sugar
½ teaspoon garlic powder
1 tablespoon sesame oil
½ tablespoon sesame seeds

Wash the leek whites. Cut them in half lengthways.

Divide the inner leaves and outer leaves into two piles. Fold each pile in half, then finely chop lengthways. Immerse the thin strips of leek in a bowl of water with a few drops of vinegar. Allow to soak for 10 minutes before draining.

Combine the leek, gochugaru, soy sauce, fermented anchovy sauce, apple vinegar, sugar, garlic powder, sesame oil and sesame seeds in a bowl. Serve.

NOTE——— *This salad is best eaten as soon as it is made. It is most often served as a garnish for Korean barbecue pork (page 166).*

MEAT &
POULTRY

Korean barbecue pork

SAMGYEOPSAL

삼 겹 살

Samgyeopsal is the Korean name for pork belly, but also refers to the preparation of barbecued pork belly and grilled vegetables. It is often eaten ssambap-style (page 156). A pork barbecue is an opportunity to gather around for a convivial meal with family or friends. A traditional or cast-iron frying pan is placed on a stove in the centre of the table or an electric grill is used to cook the meat during the meal instead of serving it already cooked. The pork can be served with leek salad (page 162), which goes well with pork and other ingredients used for ssambap. Below are some tips for organising your Korean pork belly barbecue.

SERVES 4
Preparation 10 minutes
Cooking 10 minutes

INGREDIENTS
1 kg (2 lb 4 oz) unseasoned
   pork belly, sliced
8 button mushrooms
2 saesongyi mushrooms
   (king oyster mushrooms)
1 onion
300 g (10½ oz) Chinese
   cabbage kimchi (page 90)
Ssamjang sauce
   (page 156)
Sea salt and pepper

Fried rice
2 bowls cooked white rice
   (page 10)
1 egg yolk
200 g (7 oz) Chinese
   cabbage kimchi (page 90)
A little gim seaweed (nori)
1 tablespoon sesame oil

Pork belly
Heat a cast-iron chargrill pan, frying pan or table grill. When it is hot, place the slices of pork belly on the hot pan or grill. Sprinkle with sea salt and pepper. After 3 to 5 minutes, when the blood rises on the visible side of the meat, turn over. The first side should be browned. Add the prepared vegetables (see below) around the meat. Cook for 3 to 5 minutes; when the blood rises to the surface, turn again. After 3 minutes, cut the meat with scissors. Each guest can then serve themselves.

Vegetables
Button mushrooms: Remove the stem. Place the mushroom cup upside down on the grill. When the cup fills with juice, add a little salt. Enjoy.
Saesongyi mushrooms: Cut into 5 mm (¼ inch) slices from top to bottom. Cook each side until golden brown. Eat with ssamjang sauce.
Onion: Cut into 1 cm (½ inch) thick rounds. Cook each side until golden brown. Pack in a ssam or simply dip in ssamjang sauce.
Chinese cabbage kimchi: It is eaten raw, but it can also be cooked on the grill.

Fried rice
Towards the end of the barbecue, when there are only a few ingredients left on the grill, you can end the meal by making fried rice. To do this, add the fried rice ingredients and mix them with those already on the grill. You can also add some leek salad (page 162) and fry it together with the rice if you like.

TIP —— If you want to enjoy a simple one-plate meal, cook the meat in a frying pan. Season each slice of pork belly with 1 pinch garlic powder, salt and pepper. Top with lettuce salad with kimchi sauce (page 160) and ssamjang sauce (page 156).

MEAT &
POULTRY

FISH & SEAFOOD
생선과 해산물

In Korea, the sea is a treasure trove. We eat fish in all its forms: raw, grilled, steamed or simmered. In this chapter, you will discover new ways of cooking fish with traditional as well as more modern recipes.

Grilled mackerel

GODEUNGEO-GUI

고등어구이

Mackerel is one of the most commonly eaten fish in Korea. We use it for main dishes but also as a side. It brings a uniqueness to the flavours on the table.

SERVES 4

Preparation 15 minutes
Resting 30 minutes
Cooking 40 minutes

INGREDIENTS

2 large mackerel
8 pinches coarse sea salt
4 tablespoons neutral
  vegetable oil

Gut the mackerel; cut off the head, fins and tail.

Open the belly of the fish in half by inserting a knife and sliding it along the backbone. Open out the two fillets. They must remain connected to the backbone. If traces of blood remain, scrape them lightly to remove any bitterness.

Sprinkle 2 pinches of coarse sea salt on each side of the flesh and rub gently into the fish using your hands for 2 minutes. Leave to rest for 30 minutes.

Heat a cast-iron chargrill pan or frying pan with 2 tablespoons of the vegetable oil. When it is hot, place the first fish in the pan, skin side down. Grill over a high heat for 5 minutes, covered. Reduce the heat to low and cook for another 10 minutes. When the flesh has turned white, turn the fish over. Cook again over a high heat for 5 minutes, covered. Repeat for the second fish. Serve hot.

NOTE ——— *Eat this dish with rice, beef and Chinese cabbage doenjang soup (page 142) and Chinese cabbage salad with kimchi sauce (page 114) or any type of kimchi.*

FISH &
SEAFOOD

Kimchi mackerel

GODEUNGEO KIMCHI-JORIM

고등어 김치조림

Mackerel sold in Korea are usually quite large. Choose fleshy ones and combine them in this dish with kimchi to bring out all the flavours.

SERVES 4

Preparation 20 minutes
Cooking 45 minutes

INGREDIENTS

500 g (1 lb 2 oz) mackerel
½ onion
10 cm (4 inches) leek
   (white part)
30 g (1 oz) spicy marinade
   (page 148)
25 g (1 oz) doenjang
   fermented soybean paste
2 tablespoons mat
   ganjang sauce (page 146)
1 tablespoon ginger syrup
   (page 202)
50 ml (scant ¼ cup) white
   alcohol (soju or gin)
400 g (14 oz) Chinese
   cabbage kimchi (page 90)
300 ml (1¼ cups) water

Gut the mackerel; cut off the head, fins and tail.

Cut each mackerel into three sections. Cut the onion into 1 cm (½ inch) wide slices. Cut the leek into 1 cm (½ inch) thick sections diagonally.

Prepare the sauce by mixing the spicy marinade, doenjang, mat ganjang, ginger syrup and alcohol.

Place the kimchi, without cutting it, in the bottom of a saucepan (ideally a whole ¼ cabbage). Add the mackerel pieces on top of the kimchi. Pour in the water, then the sauce, making sure the fish is well covered. Add the onion. Bring to the boil over a high heat, partially covered, then simmer for 30 minutes over a medium–low heat. Add the leek and gently mix the ingredients once only. Simmer for an additional 10 minutes.

FISH &
SEAFOOD

Fish paste

EOMUK

어묵

Eomuk is the main ingredient in many Korean dishes. It is rare to find it in the West,
so I prepare it myself in order to be able to cook my other recipes.

MAKES 500 G (1 LB 2 OZ)

Preparation 25 minutes
Cooking 20 minutes

INGREDIENTS

1 spring onion (scallion)
⅓ carrot
200 g (7 oz) raw prawns
100 g (3½ oz) squid
300 g (10½ oz) cod fillet
20 g (¾ oz) potato starch
30 g (1 oz) plain
  (all-purpose) flour
2 egg whites
1 pinch salt
1 pinch pepper
700 ml (scant 3 cups)
  neutral vegetable oil

Finely chop the spring onion and carrot. Peel the prawns and remove the veins. Gut the squid, remove the skin and clear the central beak. Purée the prawns, squid and fish together in a small food processor (**A**). Combine this mixture with the vegetables, starch, all but 1 teaspoon of the flour, the egg whites (keep the yolks to eat on a bowl of rice, mixed with soy sauce), the salt and pepper (**B**).

Heat the oil to 170°C (340°F). Sprinkle the remaining flour on a chopping board. Take about 70 g (2½ oz) of the dough and place it on the board (**C**). Using a flat steel spatula, form a cylinder with the dough by rolling it over the flour (**D**). Place the cylinder on the spatula and gently immerse it in the oil by sliding it in using a chopstick (**E**). Proceed in the same way to form more cylinders until the dough is used up. Cook each cylinder for 7 minutes, then remove from the oil and drain for a minimum of 5 minutes. Fry again in the oil for 2 minutes and allow to drain again.

Serve on a skewer with a little ketchup (**F**).

TIP —— *Fish paste can be used as an ingredient in other dishes. It can be kept for 2 days in the refrigerator. You can also freeze it.*

FISH &
SEAFOOD

A

B

C

D

E

F

Steamed sea bream

DOMI-JJIM

도미찜

SERVES 2

Preparation 30 minutes
Resting 20 minutes
Cooking 30 minutes

INGREDIENTS

1 whole sea bream, gutted

3 tablespoons white alcohol (soju or gin)

2 teaspoons sea salt

2 teaspoons ground ginger

½ teaspoon pepper

6 green leek leaves

5 g (⅛ oz) fresh ginger

½ lemon

Topping

1 medium egg

2 pyogo mushrooms (shiitake)

½ tablespoon ginger syrup (page 202)

1 tablespoon mat ganjang sauce
  (page 146)

⅔ carrot

⅓ zucchini (courgette)

½ leek (white part)

Neutral vegetable oil

Salt

Sauce

1 tablespoon soy sauce

2 tablespoons apple or apple
  cider vinegar

½ tablespoon sugar

½ teaspoon mustard

Using a knife, gently scrape the outside of the sea bream in the opposite direction to the scales to remove them. Clean the fish, carefully cleaning the tail and fins by rubbing well between two fingers. Thoroughly clean the inside and gills under running water. Mix together the soju, sea salt, ground ginger and pepper. Massage the sea bream with this marinade, inside and out. Set aside for 15 minutes.

Prepare the topping. Separate the egg white from the yolk. Season both with a little salt and beat separately. Make a thin omelette in a hot oiled frying pan with the white, then with the yolk; cut them into strips. Cut the mushrooms into matchsticks and mix with ginger syrup and mat ganjang sauce. Stir-fry for 3 minutes in a little neutral oil. Cut the carrot into matchsticks and stir-fry for 3 minutes in a little neutral oil, sprinkling with a pinch of salt. Repeat with the zucchini. Finish by shredding the white part of the leek.

Make three large cuts on each side of the sea bream at a 30-degree angle. Place a steamer basket into a Dutch oven and pour water up to 2 cm (¾ inch) below the basket. Lay the green leek leaves, sliced fresh ginger and thinly sliced lemon in the basket. Place the sea bream on top and pour the remaining marinade over. Cover and bring to the boil. Simmer for 15 minutes over a medium heat, keeping covered. Turn off the heat and stand for 5 minutes without removing the lid. Open and allow to cool for a few minutes.

Mix the sauce ingredients together. Place the sea bream on the bed of shredded white leek. Lay each of the topping ingredients on top. Eat by taking some fish flesh and topping and dipping in the sauce.

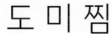

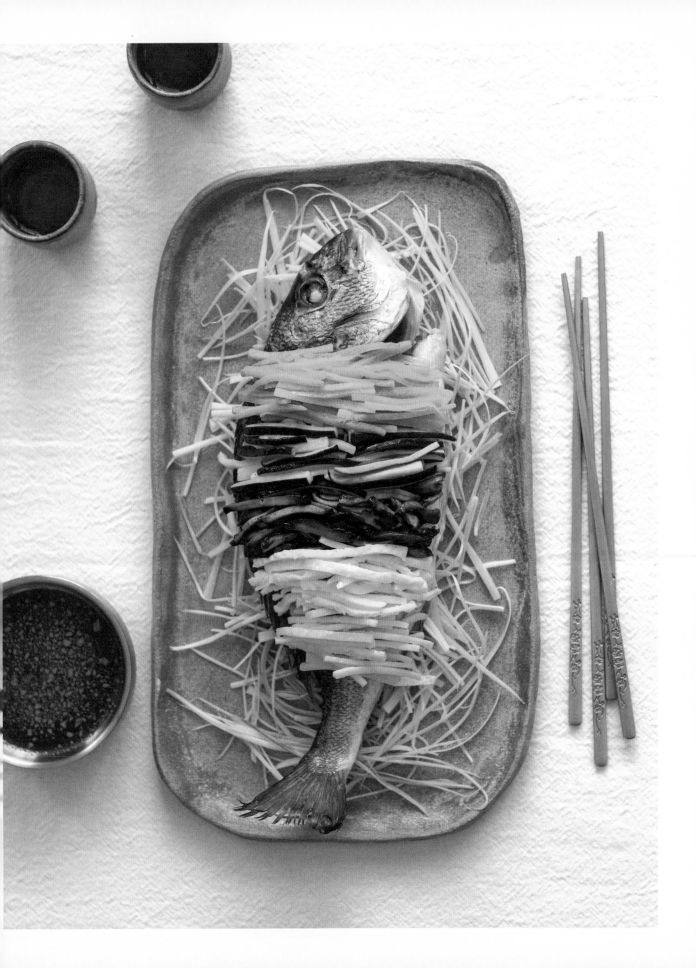

Cod rolls

SEANGSEON-MARIGUI

생 선 말 이 구 이

SERVES 2

Preparation 25 minutes
Cooking 10 minutes

INGREDIENTS

⅓ carrot

2 pyogo mushrooms
   (shiitake)

4 garlic chives

80 g (2¾ oz) bean sprouts

400 g (14 oz) cod fillet

2 tablespoons white wine

1 tablespoon ginger syrup
   (page 202)

4 tablespoons mat
   ganjang sauce
   (page 146)

1 teaspoon sesame oil

1 pinch pepper

3 tablespoons neutral
   vegetable oil

Grate the carrot. Thinly slice the mushrooms. Cut the chives into 5 cm (2 inch) pieces. Wash and drain the bean sprouts. Cut the fish into slices about 12 cm (4½ inches) long and 1 cm (½ inch) wide.

On each piece of fish, place a little carrot, a few chives, 1 mushroom slice and a few bean sprouts. Roll the fish to enclose the ingredients and secure with a small wooden toothpick.

For the marinade, mix the wine, ginger syrup, mat ganjang, sesame oil and pepper. Heat a frying pan coated with the vegetable oil over a medium heat. When the oil begins to heat, place the fish rolls into the pan. Fry for 3 minutes, turning to cook the entire surface of the rolls. Add the marinade. Simmer over a low heat for 5 minutes, turning the rolls gently so that they do not come apart.

Remove the toothpicks before serving.

FISH &
SEAFOOD

Fish fritters

SEANGSEON-TUIGIM SALAD

생선튀김 샐러드

Here is a reimagined and lighter version of fish and chips – delicious homemade fish fritters served on a small salad.

SERVES 4

Preparation 30 minutes
Cooking 10 minutes

INGREDIENTS

¼ iceberg lettuce
¼ soft lettuce
½ onion
700 g (1 lb 9 oz) white fish
2 medium eggs
80 g (2¾ oz) plain
  (all-purpose) flour
120 g (4¼ oz) panko
  breadcrumbs
1 litre (4 cups) neutral
  vegetable oil
Garlic powder
Salt and pepper

Sauce

4 tablespoons mat
  ganjang sauce
  (page 146)
2 tablespoons sugar
4 tablespoons apple or
  apple cider vinegar
3 tablespoons mineral
  water
1 pinch pepper

Wash and roughly chop the lettuces. Thinly slice the onion. Immerse the sliced onion in cold water with a few drops of vinegar for 5 minutes, then drain. Mix all the sauce ingredients together to make the sauce.

Cut the fish into rectangular pieces 3 cm (1¼ inches) thick, 5 cm (2 inches) wide and about 7 cm (2¾ inches) long. Generously sprinkle each piece with salt, pepper and garlic powder and set aside to marinate for 5 minutes. Beat the eggs. Coat each piece of fish with flour, then beaten eggs, then panko breadcrumbs.

Heat the vegetable oil to 170°C (340°F). Drop the pieces of fish into the oil and cook for 7 minutes. Carefully remove them. Place them in a colander and allow to drain for 5 minutes. Fry again for 3 minutes and drain again for 5 minutes.

Spread the salad and onion pieces on a serving dish. Drizzle with sauce. Arrange the fish fritters on top.

NOTE —— *The white fish can be replaced by salmon.*

FISH &
SEAFOOD

Squid rolls with crudités

OJINGEO-MARI

오징어말이

In Korea, this recipe of small rolls made from squid and vegetables is traditionally cooked for house-warming parties. I like to prepare it when I invite guests for pre-dinner drinks.

FOR 4 ROLLS

Preparation 25 minutes
Cooking 5 minutes

INGREDIENTS

4 squid tubes
½ red capsicum (pepper)
½ yellow capsicum (pepper)
⅓ carrot
10 cm (4 inch) piece cucumber
20 slices white radish pickles in rounds (page 122)

Spicy sauce

25 g (1 oz) gochujang chilli paste
1 tablespoon apple or apple cider vinegar
1 tablespoon sugar
1 tablespoon preserved lemon (page 198)
½ tablespoon soy sauce
1 teaspoon sesame oil
1 pinch sesame seeds

Non-spicy sauce

1 tablespoon soy sauce
½ tablespoon sugar
2 tablespoons apple or apple cider vinegar
½ teaspoon mustard
2 chives, chopped

Remove the squid tube skins and central clear beak if needed, then wash and drain. Open the tubes in half. On the outer surface of the squid, score a very tight grid pattern with a sharp knife without piercing.

Bring a pot of salted water to the boil. Immerse the squid tubes in the water. Cook for 5 minutes, then drain. Leave to cool.

Cut the capsicums and carrot into 5 mm (¼ inch) matchsticks. Using a knife, remove the central part of the cucumber with the seeds; only the outer part will be used. Cut into matchsticks.

In each squid tube arrange 5 slices of white radish pickles, some carrot, cucumber and capsicum. Close by rolling up. Pierce the roll every 2 cm (¾ inch) with toothpicks. Cut between each toothpick to make small rolls.

Mix together your choice of sauce ingredients (spicy or non-spicy) and enjoy by dipping squid rolls in the sauce.

FISH & SEAFOOD

Doenjang scallop soup

SIGEUMCHI DOENJANG-GUK

시금치 된장국

This is a simple and delicious soup made with spinach, scallops and doenjang paste, which I like to enjoy in winter to warm me up.

SERVES 4

Preparation 5 minutes
Cooking 10 minutes

INGREDIENTS

250 g (9 oz) fresh spinach
200 g (7 oz) small scallops
1.5 litres (6 cups) water, preferably from the 3rd white rice wash (page 10)
130 g (4½ oz) doenjang fermented soybean paste
4 tablespoons mat ganjang sauce (page 146)
Salt

Wash the fresh spinach thoroughly and drain. Rinse the scallops and drain.

Bring the water to the boil. Add the doenjang fermented soybean paste. When the doenjang is well dissolved, add the scallops.

As soon as boiling resumes, cook for 5 minutes, then add the spinach. Let the spinach wilt for about 3 minutes. Add the mat ganjang. Check the seasoning and add salt as needed.

FISH & SEAFOOD

DESSERTS & DRINKS
다 과

From delicious desserts, little biscuits and beautiful
rice balls to hot and cold drinks, this chapter will
introduce you to the gourmet world of sweet Korean
flavours through irresistible recipes.

Hotteok pancakes

HOTTEOK

호떡

MAKES 6 PANCAKES
Preparation 15 minutes
Resting 2 hours
Cooking 1 hour

INGREDIENTS
50 ml (scant ¼ cup) milk
200 ml (generous ¾ cup)
  water
5 g (⅛ oz) dry baker's
  yeast
15 g (½ oz) white
  (granulated) sugar
200 g (7 oz) plain
  (all-purpose) flour
70 g (2½ oz) glutinous rice
  flour
1 teaspoon salt
Neutral vegetable oil

Filling
30 g (1 oz) nut and seed
  mix: hazelnuts, walnuts,
  sunflower seeds and
  pepitas (pumpkin seeds)
60 g (2¼ oz) brown sugar
1 teaspoon ground
  cinnamon

Warm the milk and water. Combine with the yeast and white sugar. Stand for 5 minutes.

Tip the plain flour, glutinous rice flour and salt into a bowl. Add the water and milk mixture gradually, stirring after you pour in each third. Put on a pair of gloves and oil them liberally with the neutral oil, then mix the dough using your hands. The dough must be smooth and sticky. Cover and allow to stand for 2 hours at room temperature.

Crush the nuts and seeds and mix them with the brown sugar and cinnamon.

In a 9 cm (3½ inch) diameter frying pan, heat a layer of vegetable oil. Put on gloves and oil them liberally. Take a generous handful of dough in your hand (**A**). Spread it out slightly, make an indent in the middle (**B**) and add a heaped tablespoon of the nut and seed filling (**C**). Close by stretching the edges of the dough upwards to cover the filling (**D**).

Place the filled dough in the frying pan. Press gently with an oiled metal pusher (or use an oiled spatula) to obtain a round shape without piercing the dough (**E**). Turn over halfway through cooking or after about 5 minutes. Both sides should be nicely golden brown. Make 6 pancakes in total and serve (**F**).

DESSERTS
& DRINKS

A

B

C

D

E

F

Matcha and white chocolate hotteok pancakes

NOKCHA-HOTTEOK

녹차 호떡

Once you have learnt the technique for this recipe, have fun playing with the flavour of the dough and your choice of favourite fillings, especially with the quality chocolates you can now find in stores.

MAKES 6 PANCAKES

Preparation 15 minutes
Resting 2 hours
Cooking 1 hour

INGREDIENTS

200 ml (generous ¾ cup) water
5 g (⅛ oz) dry baker's yeast
25 g white (granulated) sugar
50 ml (scant ¼ cup) milk
2 tablespoons matcha green tea powder
200 g (7 oz) plain (all-purpose) flour
70 g (2½ oz) glutinous rice flour
1 teaspoon salt
Neutral vegetable oil

Filling

50 g (1¾ oz) white cooking chocolate
30 g (1 oz) hazelnuts
⅓ teaspoon vanilla powder

Warm the water, add the yeast and white sugar, then mix together. Stand for 5 minutes. Warm the milk, add the matcha powder and mix. Mix the matcha milk with the sweetened water with the yeast.

Tip the plain flour, glutinous rice flour and salt into a bowl Pour in the water and matcha milk mixture gradually, stirring after you pour in each third. Put on a pair of gloves and oil them liberally with the neutral oil, then mix the dough using your hands. The dough must be smooth and sticky. Cover and allow to stand for 2 hours at room temperature.

Cut the white chocolate into pieces and crush the hazelnuts. Combine the chocolate, hazelnuts and vanilla powder.

In a 9 cm (3½ inch) diameter frying pan, heat a layer of vegetable oil. Put on gloves and oil them liberally. Take a generous handful of dough in your hand. Spread it out slightly, make an indent in the middle and add a heaped tablespoon of the hazelnut-chocolate filling. Close by stretching the edges of the dough upwards to cover the filling.

Place the filled dough in the frying pan. Press gently with an oiled metal pusher (or use an oiled spatula) to obtain a round shape without piercing the dough. Turn over halfway through cooking or after about 5 minutes. Both sides should be nicely golden brown. Make 6 pancakes in total, perhaps serving with a scoop of vanilla ice-cream and some berries.

DESSERTS
& DRINKS

Sweet rice balls

GYEONGDAN

경단

This is the first recipe I learnt to cook when I was in high school in Korea. Vary the flavours of these cute little glutinous rice balls to your liking. I recommend enjoying them with a nice hot cup of tea.

FOR 25 BALLS
Preparation 40 minutes
Resting 10 minutes
Cooking 10 minutes

INGREDIENTS
200 g (7 oz) glutinous rice flour
½ teaspoon salt
30 g (1 oz) white (granulated) sugar
100–150 ml (approx. ½ cup) boiling water
30 g (1 oz) sponge finger biscuits
5 g (⅛ oz) matcha green tea powder
5 g (⅛ oz) chocolate powder
5 g (⅛ oz) purple sweet potato powder
125 g (4½ oz) sweet red bean paste (anko)
30 g (1 oz) potato starch

Tip the glutinous rice flour, salt and 10 g (¼ oz) of the sugar into a bowl. Gradually add the boiling water to the bowl in stages, using a tablespoon to mix together first, then using your hands with each addition as it cools. Ensure that the water always remains boiling and repeat this process until you obtain a thick, smooth dough, like playdough. Once it is smooth, knead it vigorously for 5 minutes. Cover the dough with a damp tea towel and stand for 10 minutes at room temperature.

Crush the biscuits with a spoon through a fine mesh sieve to make a fine powder. Mix 10 g (¼ oz) of the biscuit powder with the matcha, 10 g (¼ oz) with the chocolate powder and 10 g (¼ oz) with the sweet potato powder.

Divide the dough into 12 g (½ oz) portions. Make small balls. Press in the centre of each ball to form an indent and fill with 5 g (⅛ oz) red bean paste. Close the ball over the paste and roll each ball in the potato starch.

Immerse the balls in a saucepan of boiling water. As soon as they rise to the surface, wait 2 minutes, then scoop them up using a skimmer. Place them in a bowl of cold water, then in a second bowl of cold water. Drain and roll in the remaining 20 g (¾ oz) sugar.

Roll the balls, one at a time, in the powder of your choice: chocolate, matcha or sweet potato.

DESSERTS & DRINKS

Dalgona biscuits

DALGONA

달 고 나

In Korea, this sweet used to be prepared at small stands outside schools. If children were able to separate the shape from the rest of the biscuit without breaking it, they were given a free sweet by the stallholders as a reward.

FOR 1 BISCUIT
Preparation 5 minutes
Cooking 5 minutes

INGREDIENTS
2 tablespoons white sugar
¼ teaspoon bicarbonate of soda (baking soda)

Pour the sugar into a stainless steel ladle. Light a gas burner and hold the ladle over it. Mix the sugar with a disposable wooden chopstick, raising and lowering the ladle while mixing to control the temperature without burning.

When the sugar is melted but not boiling, add the bicarbonate of soda and move a little further away from the heat. Mix vigorously to obtain a puffy beige paste. When a caramel aroma emerges, mix for another 20 seconds and then pour the mixture in one or two pours onto a baking sheet covered with baking paper. Discard the remaining caramel stuck in the ladle. Wait 20 seconds, then press the dough with a round metal cookie cutter. Carefully remove the cutter after 5 seconds. Please note that the waiting times may vary depending on the ambient temperature. The times given here are based on a room temperature of approximately 20°C (68°F).

To print the shape, use a cookie cutter of your choice, gently pressing it onto the biscuit just after removing the round cutter.

DESSERTS
& DRINKS

Yakgwa biscuits

YAKGWA

약 과

*When I visited my grandmother as a little girl, I loved going to her room. She always opened
her drawer to offer me a yakgwa, which I would hold between my little hands like a treasure.*

FOR 20 BISCUITS
Preparation 30 minutes
Resting 24 hours
Cooking 20 minutes

INGREDIENTS
*1 litre (4 cups) neutral
vegetable oil*
20 sunflower seeds
*20 pepitas (pumpkin
seeds)*
5 dried jujubes

Jip-cheong syrup
5 g (⅛ oz) fresh ginger
320 g (11¼ oz) rice syrup
50 g (1¾ oz) honey
*100 ml (scant ½ cup)
water*

Batter
*200 g (7 oz) plain
(all-purpose) flour*
½ tablespoon sesame oil
1 teaspoon salt
1 pinch pepper
*1 teaspoon ground
cinnamon*
75 g (2½ oz) brown sugar
2 tablespoons water
*1 tablespoon neutral
vegetable oil*

For the jip-cheong syrup, peel the ginger. Combine the rice syrup, honey, water and peeled ginger in a saucepan. Heat over a medium heat. When it starts to boil and the syrup begins to rise, reduce the heat to low and cook for 5 minutes. Discard the ginger pieces and set aside.

To make the batter, tip the flour into a mixing bowl and scatter the sesame oil in drops on top. Rub in the drops with your fingertips to distribute them throughout the flour. Sift the flour with a fine mesh sieve, using a spoon to help it through. Mix the sifted flour with the salt, pepper and cinnamon. In a bowl, dissolve the sugar in the water, stirring regularly for 10 minutes. Add to the flour, along with 1½ tablespoons of the jip-cheong syrup and the neutral vegetable oil. Use the edge of a spatula to combine, sliding it from one edge of the bowl to the other, down to the bottom of the bowl. When the mixture is well combined, form a ball using your hands (be careful not to overmix to prevent the dough from becoming too elastic).

Roll the dough out to 1 cm (½ inch) thick on a chopping board using a rolling pin. Cut out biscuits using a 3.5 cm (1½ inch) diameter cookie cutter. Before removing the cutter, press lightly in the middle of the biscuit with your finger. Prick the surface 10 times with a toothpick and remove the cookie cutter.

Heat the vegetable oil in a wok over a medium heat. Use your hand to check the temperature by positioning it above the oil. When the heat starts to rise slightly, place the dough pieces into the oil. If the biscuits stick to the bottom or to each other, peel them off very gently. When the biscuits rise to the surface, increase the heat to high. Remove them from the oil as soon as they are golden brown and immediately immerse them in the remaining jip-cheong syrup. Leave to rest at room temperature for at least 6 hours.

Place the biscuits on a rack. Decorate with the seeds and jujube flowers, adding a few drops of jip-cheong syrup to the decorations to stick them. Leave to dry until the next day. The drying is complete when the syrup does not stick to your fingers too much.

TIP —— *To make the jujube flowers, insert a knife at an angle along the length of the jujube. Turn as you cut to keep only the outer part. Line the flesh side with syrup and roll up tightly. Cut into thin slices.*

DESSERTS
& DRINKS

Preserved lemon

LEMON-CHEONG

레몬청

This Korean preserved lemon is ideal for making cold drinks, salad dressings or marinades.

FOR A 500 ML (17 FL OZ) JAR
Preparation 30 minutes

INGREDIENTS
8 to 10 lemons
1 lime
330 g (11½ oz) white (granulated) sugar
Bicarbonate of soda (baking soda)

Rinse the lemons and lime with water. Rub the wet skins well with the bicarbonate of soda, then rinse them again. Squeeze enough lemons to obtain 300 ml (1¼ cups) juice. Mix the juice with the sugar and stir until the sugar has dissolved.

Cut 1 or 2 lemons and the lime into very thin slices. Mix the slices with the sugared lemon juice. Pour the mixture into a sterilised jar (page 118).

This preserved lemon keeps for 3 months in the refrigerator.

DESSERTS
& DRINKS

Homemade lemonade

LEMONADE

레 몬 에 이 드

This is my preferred drink in Korea. There is a perfect balance between sweet and sour in this recipe. From the first sip, you can taste the citrusy freshness in your mouth.

**MAKES 1 GLASS
(330 ML/11¼ FL OZ)**

Plain lemonade
Place 3 tablespoons preserved lemon juice (page 198) and a slice of preserved lemon into a glass. Pour 250 ml (1 cup) cold sparkling water into the glass and mix gently.

Berry lemonade
Roughly crush 10 raspberries at the bottom of a glass. Add 3 tablespoons preserved lemon juice (page 198) and a slice of preserved lemon. Pour 250 ml (1 cup) cold sparkling water into the glass and mix gently.

Mint lemonade
Roughly tear a few mint leaves to release the flavour and place them at the bottom of a glass. Add 3 tablespoons perserved lemon juice (page 198) and a slice of preserved lemon. Pour 250 ml (1 cup) cold sparkling water into the glass and mix gently.

DESSERTS
& DRINKS

Ginger syrup

SAENGGANG-CHEONG

생 강 청

I always have a small jar of ginger syrup in my refrigerator. In addition to the medicinal virtues of this root, I like to add some to a cup of tea to enhance the taste.

FOR A 500 ML (17 FL OZ) JAR

Preparation 40 minutes
Resting 2 hours
Cooking 50 minutes

INGREDIENTS

1 kg (2 lb 4 oz) fresh
  ginger, skin on
1 pear
500 g (1 lb 2 oz) raw sugar

Soak the ginger roots in cold water and stand for 30 minutes to make them easy to peel. Peel the ginger roots completely by scraping the widest parts with a small spoon and using a small knife for the corners. Peel and remove the core from the pear.

Process the ginger and pear together in a small food processor until smooth. Place a fine mesh sieve over a bowl. Line the sieve with a cotton muslin bag, pour in the ginger mixture and close the bag. Press it with a ladle to draw out as much juice as possible. Discard the contents of the bag and set the bowl with the juice aside for 1½ hours.

Pour the juice into a saucepan very gently, taking care not to pour in the starch that remains at the bottom of the bowl. Add the sugar and heat, uncovered, over a low to medium heat for 50 minutes, stirring regularly.

Leave to cool slightly, then pour into a sterilised jar (page 118). Place in the refrigerator once cooled.

Ginger syrup keeps for 3 months in the refrigerator.

DESSERTS
& DRINKS

Ginger drinks

SAENGGANG-EUMLYO

생강음료

Ginger tea

FOR 1 CUP
Preparation 5 minutes

INGREDIENTS
330 ml (1⅓ cups) water, 2 tablespoons ginger syrup (page 202)

Boil the water and mix with the ginger syrup.

Ginger latte

FOR 1 CUP
Preparation 5 minutes

INGREDIENTS
330 ml (1⅓ cups) milk, 2 tablespoons ginger syrup (page 202), ground cinnamon

Heat the milk without boiling it. Mix it with the ginger syrup. Sprinkle with cinnamon.

DESSERTS
& DRINKS

RESOURCES

Basic ingredients

Gochujang – fermented chilli paste —— This spicy soybean paste is one of the basic ingredients to have in your kitchen. It is used in many Korean dishes and can be kept in the refrigerator for a long time.

Doenjang – fermented soybean paste —— This Korean fermented soybean paste is commonly used for making many soups and marinades. It is easily found in stores, including online, and can be kept for several months in the refrigerator.

Gochugaru – chilli powder —— This powder is made with red chilli flakes. It is essential for properly balancing the seasoning of spicy dishes, or to add a slightly spicy taste, just like pepper is used in other cuisines.

Sesame oil —— Korean sesame oil is a toasted sesame oil with a subtle taste. In the absence of a Korean oil, choose a Japanese toasted sesame oil rather than those from other countries, which are generally less pungent.

Soy sauce —— This dark soy sauce is essential for a wide variety of dishes and seasonings. If you don't use Korean soy sauce, any other Asian brand of soy sauce will do, but it is best to choose low-salt sauces.

Fermented anchovy sauce —— Anchovy sauce is a basic ingredient that is found more and more easily outside of Korea. It is to Korean cuisine what nuoc-mam (fish sauce) is to Vietnamese cuisine. In the absence of anchovy sauce, you can replace it with nuoc-mam, even though the taste will be slightly different.

Soju —— This Korean white alcohol has a neutral taste and is good for tenderising meats and removing the 'meaty' smell, which is considered unpleasant in Korean cuisine. If you do not have any soju, replace it with the same quantity of gin.

Apple vinegar —— This Korean vinegar adds flavour to many sauces. The logical alternative is apple cider vinegar that will bring the spice of vinegar and the scent of apple to your dishes.

Rice syrup —— Rice syrup is mainly used in desserts to add shine and texture.

Corn syrup —— Corn syrup is used in some dishes instead of sugar, especially for its texture, which is good for coating. Otherwise, honey can be used although it will give a less neutral taste. Agave syrup is also a possible alternative.

Toasted sesame seeds —— Sesame seeds are a condiment usually added at the end of seasoning or used in some desserts. They are used whole or crushed, depending on the dish. They can be light brown or black and the colour chosen depends on what visual effect is desired. In terms of taste, regardless of the brand used, pay attention to the quality of manufacture. Choose a Korean brand or organic alternatives, especially if you eat them regularly.

Korean curry powder —— There is only one curry mix in Korea. It was created and is still sold by the Ottogi® brand. Curry is a mixture of spices introduced to Korean cooking in the twentieth century, which has rapidly become part of many different cuisines.

Chunjang – black bean paste —— Chunjang is an ingredient that comes from northeast China. In Korea, it is included in dishes using jjajang sauce, with chunjang being the main ingredient. It exists in two versions: an uncooked one that requires stir-frying before use (which I recommend), and a precooked one that will not need to be fried. You must pay attention to the type you buy before using it in cooking.

Dangmyeon – sweet potato vermicelli —— These typically Korean vermicelli have an elastic texture. Alternatively, use Vietnamese mung bean vermicelli, which have a similar taste, even if their texture is slightly different. However, only soak them for 1 hour in water before cooking, unlike the 2 hours needed for Korean dangmyeon.

Somyeon noodles —— These very fine wheat noodles can be eaten hot, but are also used in many cold Korean noodle dishes. To use them successfully, the cooking technique of cooling them several times must be followed to remove the starch. They are also known as the Japanese 'somen' noodles.

Dried jujujubes —— Dried jujubes, or Chinese dates, are used as an ingredient as well as to garnish dishes.

Firm tofu —— Firm tofu is used in many dishes, either as a main ingredient or as part of a broth, for example. It is consumed cold, heated, simply pan-fried or boiled. Avoid European industrial brands, which generally lack taste.

Miyeok seaweed ——— Generally sold dried, this seaweed is perfect for certain soups and salads, once rehydrated. It is also known as the Japanese 'wakame'.

Gim seaweed ——— This seaweed is also known as nori and comes in two forms. First of all its plain version in large sheets, which can be used to roll gimbap (page 116). Secondly, it is sold in the form of small seasoned seaweed sheets that can be consumed without preparation as a side to a dish. For Koreans, this variety is one of their favourite side dishes. You can simply fill the sheet with rice, some cabbage kimchi or any other side to suit everyone's tastes.

Asian white radish (daikon) ——— Asian white radishes can come in all sizes and shapes. Outside Korea, they are most often found in their very long form. If you cannot find white radishes, a large black radish or even turnips can replace them in many recipes.

Glutinous rice flour ——— This type of flour is very often used for desserts, kimchi and occasionally in dough to give a more elastic texture. There are two types of rice flour: glutinous and non-glutinous. The first is usually easier to find than the second, so the recipes in this book do not use the second.

Utensils

No special utensils are needed to cook Korean food at home.
I bought all the utensils used in this book in major stores or online.

Cast-iron pan ——— This coating is ideal for all grilled marinated meats, especially if the meat is cooked directly at the table as a barbecue. It can be replaced by any large, traditional frying pan or a tabletop grill.

Small frying pan ——— I love a small 9 cm (3½ inch) diameter frying pan. Not only does it allow me to make small, perfectly round pancakes, but also nice round fried eggs to serve on top of some dishes.

Wide sauté pan ——— A wide sauté pan or a wok is very useful for Korean cuisine.

Dutch oven ——— A cast-iron Dutch oven, or even a large saucepan, is essential for making rice and simmered dishes. The most important thing is that it has a lid.

Fine mesh sieve ——— A fine mesh sieve/strainer allows you to drain fried food, strain syrups or infuse ingredients for a broth.

Mortar and pestle ——— A wooden mortar and pestle make it easy to crush sesame seeds.

Cotton muslin bag ——— This re-usable bag allows you to infuse or strain a large amount of ingredients for certain broths. I love it because it's practical and environmentally friendly.

Mandolin ——— A mandolin makes many types of cuts easy. It is epecially good for very thin slices and the thin matchsticks often used in Korean cuisine (bigger than grated but not too big), for example for white radish when making kimchi.

Skimmer ——— I often use this between two rounds of frying in oil to prevent burnt residues from spoiling the taste and appearance of fritters. It is also handy when boiling beef to remove fat without using a colander.

Chef's knife ——— A large knife with a wide blade is very convenient for cutting many vegetables. It is especially useful for chopping very finely.

Large thin knife ——— This knife is ideal for cutting meat and poultry, provided it is very well sharpened.

Scissors ——— In the West we are more likely to find scissors in school pencil cases, but in Korea it is in the kitchen that they find their place. Use for cutting kimchi, chicken skin, pork belly and chives etc. This is an essential utensil for me.

Garlic crusher ——— The number one ingredient in Korean cuisine is garlic. A metal garlic crusher is essential to avoid spending hours chopping it finely by hand.

Metal pusher ——— This small pusher is perfect for shaping pancakes and some desserts.

Whisk ——— Some Korean batters are thick and sticky, so buy a good-quality whisk if you don't want it to break. Unfortunately, silicone whisks are not compatible with these textures.

Chopsticks ——— For making Korean cuisine, there is nothing better than chopsticks, especially to sauté meat and vegetables and deftly reposition an ingredient that is out of place during cooking. They are also very practical for getting garnishes just right.

Pastry brush ——— A pastry brush is your best friend when it comes to spreading the right amount of sauce on fragile ingredients or coating ingredients with certain sauces.

Flat steel spatula ——— I use this to shape certain dishes or smooth the sauce in a single spread.

Metal tongs ——— I often use these together with scissors to cut ingredients. I also find them useful for turning meat on the barbecue, separating food or removing items from oil when frying.

Recipe list

RICE | NOODLES, PANCAKES & FRITTERS | VEGETABLES | KIMCHI & PICKLES | MEAT & POULTRY | FISH & SEAFOOD | DESSERTS & DRINKS

Ingredients index

Acknowledgements

Thank you first of all to my husband Cyril Canac, who supported and encouraged me throughout the creation of this book.

Thank you to my mum for everything, for being there for me and for sharing her family recipes, without which I would never have developed my love for cooking. I love you mum!

Thanks to Yena and Lena who were with me every step of the way in making this book. My little sisters, you are the sunshine in my life.

Thank you to all my French in-laws, the Canac family. It is thanks to you that I adapt my Korean cuisine to Western practices and allow more people to get to know it.

Thank you to my friends Myeongju and Rayoung, who willingly agreed to be part of the Korean barbecue photo shoot.

Thank you to Akiko Ida, photographer of this book. You were like a big sister to me, always making me feel at ease. Thank you for your magnificent work.

Thank you to my editor Galatéa Pedroche, who entrusted me with the freedom to make this book as I liked.

Thanks to Christine Légeret for setting authentic Korean tables.

Finally, thank you to all those who support me on my Jay's KFOOD Youtube channel and my Instagram account @jay_cuisine_corenne!

Ingredients Shopping:
ACE MART: 63, rue Sainte-Anne, 75002 Paris
ACE Boucherie: 58, rue Sainte-Anne, 75002 Paris acemartmall.com

Styling Shopping:
Atelier Lande - Cécile Gaudey: cecilegaudey.com
Chiche Ceramiques – Émilie Chaillou: Instagram: @chicheceramiques
Nous Paris: nousparis.com

Published in 2023 by Murdoch Books, an imprint of Allen & Unwin
First published in 2022 by Hachette Livre (Marabout)

Murdoch Books Australia
Cammeraygal Country
83 Alexander Street
Crows Nest NSW 2065
Phone: +61 (0)2 8425 0100
murdochbooks.com.au
info@murdochbooks.com.au

Murdoch Books UK
Ormond House
26–27 Boswell Street
London WC1N 3JZ
Phone: +44 (0) 20 8785 5995
murdochbooks.co.uk
info@murdochbooks.co.uk

For corporate orders and custom publishing, contact our business development team at salesenquiries@murdochbooks.com.au

Photography: Akiko Ida
Styling: Christine Légeret
Layout: Jérôme Cousin and Nicolas Galy for NoOok
Proofreading: Natacha Kotchetkova

Publisher: Jane Morrow
Translator: Nicola Thayil
English-language editor: Kay Halsey
English-language designer and cover designer: Sarah McCoy
Production Director: Lou Playfair

ISBN 978 1 92261 692 0

A catalogue record for this book is available from the National Library of Australia

A catalogue record for this book is available from the British Library

Printed by C & C Offset Printing Co. Ltd., China

IMPORTANT: Those who might be at risk from the effects of salmonella poisoning (the elderly, pregnant women, young children and those suffering from immune deficiency diseases) should consult their doctor with any concerns about eating raw eggs. Please ensure that all seafood and beef to be eaten raw or lightly cooked are very fresh and of the highest quality.

TABLESPOON MEASURES: We have used 15 ml (3 teaspoon) tablespoon measures.

10 9 8 7 6 5 4 3 2 1